YOUR NEW POWERBOAT:
CHOOSING IT, USING IT

The Editors of Chapman Piloting

Hearst Books
A Division of Sterling Publishing Co., Inc.
New York

Every effort has been made to ensure that all the information in this book is accurate. However, due to differing conditions, tools, and individual skills, the publisher cannot be responsible for any injuries, losses, and other damages that may result from the use of the information in this book.

Produced by JaBS MEDIA, a division of Bill Smith Studio
Publisher: Jacqueline A. Ball
Art & Design: Jay Jaffe, Brad Holroyd
Production Director: Maureen O'Connor
Production: Jeanine Colgan

Library of Congress Cataloging-in-Publication Data
Your new powerboat / edited by Diana B. Jessie ; Roger Marshall, contributor.
p.cm. — (A Chapman nautical guide)
ISBN 1-58816-083-1
Motorboats. I. Jessie, Diana. II. Marshall, Roger. III. Series.

VM341.Y67 2002
623.8'231 — dc21   2001039866

10 9 8 7 6 5 4 3 2 1

Published by Hearst Books, a division of
Sterling Publishing Company, Inc.
387 Park Avenue South, New York, N.Y. 10016

CHAPMAN and CHAPMAN PILOTING and Hearst Books are trademarks
owned by Hearst Communications, Inc.

Distributed in Canada by Sterling Publishing
c/o Canadian Manda Group, One Atlantic Avenue, Suite 105
Toronto, Ontario, Canada M6K 3E7
Distributed in Australia by Capricorn Link (Australia) Pty. Ltd.
P.O. Box 704, Windsor, NSW 2756 Australia

Printed in the United States of America

ISBN 1-58816-083-1

Introduction and Acknowledgments

Whether this is your first boat, or your second—or even your third or fourth—*Your New Powerboat: Choosing It, Using It* will guide you through the process of selecting and purchasing the powerboat that's exactly right for you. Whether "new" means really new or used—for there are great bargains to be had in used boats—*Your New Powerboat* offers comprehensive guidelines on what to look for in a boat and how to use it for maximum enjoyment. If you've been dreaming of a powerboat for family fun, racing, or cruising, all the information you need is right here in these pages.

This is the only reference guide that can take buyers in all budget ranges and of all backgrounds and experience through the process of finding their own dreamboats. Throughout the book, you'll have the chance to assess your desires, needs, financial means, and abilities, so you can narrow down the myriad of choices available to you. And after you've made your purchase, *Your New Powerboat* shows you how to maintain your boat in "Bristol fashion" for maximum resale value.

Your New Powerboat comes with the accuracy and authority that have become synonymous with *Chapman Piloting,* the premier name in marine publishing. In these pages, you'll find detailed descriptions of boats of all makes, sizes, and construction. In addition, there's advice from the experts on everything from when to use a surveyor to stocking a galley to choosing the right anchor. You'll also find all the safety procedures you're required to follow as prescribed by the U.S. Coast Guard.

Handy charts, checklists, and diagrams in each chapter make boating information accessible at a glance and allows you to develop customized maintenance schedules and safety checklists. You'll also find helpful website addresses and phone numbers for boating manufacturers and powerboating organizations. Tips throughout offer special insights and some common-sense wisdom from experienced boaters.

This book isn't just a how-to book for boat buying, nor is it just about the mechanics of owning and safely operating a powerboat. It's about *boating*: boating as part of your lifestyle; what you can do with the boat after it's yours; how to use it responsibly while having the most fun with it. It will teach you to be a better boater by building upon the expertise you already have.

Contributors to this book include Diana B. Jessie, Jim Jessie, and Ruth Ashby. Special thanks to Roger Marshall, yacht designer, author, and Technical Editor with *Soundings.* Others who supplied valuable information are Dauntless Marina (Essex, CT); Sheila and Bob Gunther; John Ball; and Leslie Quarrier, yacht broker (Old Lyme, CT).

Note: All price ranges cited are as of 2002.

TABLE OF CONTENTS

PART I

THE
DREAM

For many people, buying a boat is the realization of a dream. Boating is one of the few recreational pursuits that your entire family can enjoy. Not only can you enjoy the breeze in your face on a warm sunny day, you can fish, swim, water ski, wakeboard, sleep and eat aboard, explore new places, and meet new people. With the right boat, you can even visit different countries. In short, boating allows you to have quality time with your family and to relax on the water.

CHAPTER 1

ASK
YOURSELF...

The first step when buying a boat is to think about what you want to do with the boat, where you want to go, and how much it is going to cost. A boat represents a major investment of your time, energy, and money. Only you can decide which boat is best for you. The best place to start is by asking yourself: **How am I going to use my new powerboat?**

If you have never been out in a powerboat, **take a course.** In a recent U.S. Coast Guard (USCG) report, over 84% of the people who had boating accidents had not taken any boating courses. Beginning boaters can take courses from the Auxiliary or the U.S. Power Squadron. Call 1-800-336-BOAT to find out about boating classes in your area. You will especially need to take a course if you want to own a high-speed boat. Some manufacturers, such as Wellcraft, have schools for just that.

With a course or two under your belt, ask yourself: Am I going to use my boat to fish? Cruise to a nice spot and picnic aboard? Take the kids waterskiing? Race or participate in predicted log events? Although the same boat can be used for each of these activities, if you decide to specialize, you will need a boat that suits what you plan to do most of the time. You might decide that for now you will take the family boating, but in a couple of years when the kids have gone to college, you'll want to go sportfishing. That's a good goal to have, but don't buy a boat today for tomorrow's needs. Buy a family boat and trade it later. Think of your needs right now.

Do you want to use your boat for family activities? Powerboating is a great family activity. No other sport, except sailing, allows everybody in the family to enjoy working and playing together. The opportunity to learn self-sufficiency through boating together is a great lesson for family members.

Do you want to live aboard? Living on a boat is appealing to many people. In a temperate climate, it can be a very pleasant experience. However, not having to mow the lawn doesn't mean your life will be free of maintenance. You will have to maintain the boat if you intend to resell it. Maintenance can be a big expense unless you do most of it yourself. Fortunately, most of the maintenance can be done at the end of the season or over the winter when the boat is hauled out. Finding a place to keep a boat that you can live on can be both difficult and costly. Many states tax live-aboards and some are making laws against living aboard boats. The bright spot is that some marinas encourage live-aboards because they provide a presence that keeps crime down.

TIP
If you generally plan to cruise for longer than a day with other adults, you'll need at least one semi-private area per person or couple.

If you plan to **live aboard** your boat, check with the local government and marina operator to find out if you can live aboard before you buy the boat. Living aboard a boat is better than having a second home because you can go somewhere else when the scenery gets boring, and you still get the tax breaks of a second home.

The Number 1 Question: Budget?

Before you go any further, you need to consider your budget. There's no point picking a 40-foot trawler-style cruiser such as an Albin or a Grand Banks if you cannot afford to put fuel in it. If your budget is limited, you should look at a used boat. If your budget is *really* limited, look at a smaller boat and trade up later. Generally, used boats come with equipment that you would otherwise have to buy for a new boat. Many new boats drop dramatically in value as soon as you drive them off the dealer's lot. A look in any boating magazine will give you a quick picture of what is available in your price range. However, it is important to remember that the initial cost of the boat is only the beginning.

What can you get for your money?

Boats vary tremendously in quality, style, and durable accessories. For a few hundred dollars and a lot of work, you might be able to get a small fishing boat, but if you have aspirations for a larger boat, you need to have cash or credit. Here's a rough guide to what you might expect to pay.

Can you spend...less than $10,000?

If you plan to spend less than $10,000, you will find the market limited to small open boats less than 16 feet in length. A larger boat that is a fixer-upper and may not have an engine can also be bought for this price. But your boat will probably offer limited use and space and not much comfort.

Between $10,000 and $20,000?

If you can spend between $10,000 and $20,000, you will find a selection of used boats in the 20-foot range. Most boats of this size will be trailerable and are usually offered with a trailer. If your purchase price includes the cost of the trailer, you will save money in berth or storage fees. This size range is practical for inshore use, although skilled boaters often take them a little further offshore. A boat in this range will be limited in amenities, although some of the latest boats have a center console with an enclosed head and cuddy cabin (a small enclosed area in the bow of the boat). The engine is likely to be an outboard of up to 100 horsepower. Typical boats in this price range are a 1981 Grady-White for $12,500, a 1980 Pursuit for $14,900.

Can you spend...between $20,000 and $30,000?

If this is your budget, the range of boats you can afford will include some brand new, open trailerable boats, as well as some good used ones. For example, a 24-foot 1989 Formula was recently advertised for $22,000. Old wooden boats may be bigger and require a lot of restoration work and possibly new engines (a major expense). Used ski boats and fishing boats are available in this price range, too.

Between $30,000 and $50,000?

In this range, your choices expand even further. The size range in this budget category will largely be limited to sportfishing boats of up to 30 feet, trawler yachts, and cruisers of around 25 to 30 feet, and older boats that might be slightly larger (but will require more work).

> ⚓ **T I P**
>
> Whatever first boat you buy, think of it as the first in a series of upgrades. It may be wiser to spend a little less initially and discover what features are most important to you.

Between $50,000 and $100,000?

If you have up to $100,000 to spend on your boat, you can get a reasonably sized sportfishing boat or one of a limited range of inshore cruisers. In a recent issue of *Soundings Boats for Sale*, one of the best sources for used boats, there was a 32-foot Carver 1986 listed for $54,000; a 32-foot 1996 Bayliner for $64,000; and a 32-foot 1995 Luhrs for $103,000. Note that you can look at boats up to $120,000 in this range, because you will usually bid lower than the asking price and negotiate with the owner.

Over $100,000?

When your budget exceeds $100,000, it's a good idea to consult a yacht broker. You will be able to look at a variety of new and used boats of varying sizes. Larger boats will cost considerably more. For example, a used 78-foot 1976 Hatteras may list for $995,000. Such a boat may cost $2 to $3 million when new.

The purchasing decision comes down to what you want to do with your boat. If you want to go sportfishing, a fully tricked out, top of the line, 33-foot Black Watch can cost over $200,000 used and nearly $300,000 new. An older, not so highly regarded 1978 32-footer by a different manufacturer can be purchased for $39,900. But the older boat may have twin gas engines that may need repair. If you want to go cruising with your family, a 33-foot 1994 SeaRay for $80,000 or an older Carver 1981 for $38,000 would both be appropriate.

The size of a boat affects where you can go, how long you can stay out, the number of people you can have aboard, and how much gear you can bring along. If you intend to go for a weekend with your family, you will need a boat around 22 to 26 feet long to be reasonably comfortable.

Can it be...14 feet or less?

A 14-foot or less boat is suitable for sheltered bays and harbors. Many boats of this size have a center console or cuddy cabin, while others are totally open. Newer boats may have a cramped, enclosed toilet unit in the center console or cuddy. You should pick your weather carefully before going out of sight of land in such a small boat. Safety considerations dictate that personal flotation gear must be worn whenever using a boat of this size. Some small boats, such as a Boston Whaler, have flotation built into the boat. A boat of this size will almost certainly have an outboard engine of up to 25 hp.

15 to 20 feet?

15 to 20 feet gives you a little more roaming room, but not much. This size range is very popular for inshore fishing, commuting across harbors, water-skiing, and wakeboarding. Amenities are limited to a toilet in the cuddy cabin or center console, and possibly a small bunk in the cuddy cabin. A boat of this size will generally have an outboard engine of up to 100 hp.

21 to 26 feet?

This size can take you 8 to 10 miles offshore, but you will need to keep an eye on the weather, and head for home if the weather degrades. You can go further offshore, but not without filing a float plan with the U.S. Coast Guard and having a fast enough boat to get you home quickly.

In this size range, most of your usable space is open deck, although some of the cruising boats have a double berth under the cockpit, a galley forward, and even a small dinette. However, they may lack full standing head-room. This is the most popular size range and offers greater variety and styles than any other. The boat may have single or twin outboard engines, although some cruisers have stern drives.

Can it be...27 to 32 feet?

At 27 feet and more, you start to get into boats that have full standing headroom. In a boat of this size that is well built and reasonably fast you can go out of sight of land, but should still keep an eye on the weather. Boats of this size range can have inboard engines, outboards (usually a twin engine installation), or a stern drive. Sportfishing boats will have an enclosed cabin forward, usually with two or four bunks, an enclosed toilet, and a small galley. In addition, a cruiser may have a double bunk in an enclosed cabin under the cockpit.

32 to 40 feet?

In this range you can have a boat that you can really enjoy—comfortably live aboard, transit the Intracoastal, or go offshore. For many people this is about the largest boat they can handle alone. Some trawler yachts fit right into this range and have two cabins with double bunks forward and aft and with en suite toilets, twin inboard engines driving twin props, and a large, comfortable dining saloon with a well-equipped galley.

High-speed hulls have similar facilities but a very different hull shape. Sportfishing boats of this size can go out to the canyons (located about 40 to 50 miles offshore on the edge of the Atlantic continental shelf) to fish for tuna and other large fish. A sportfishing boat may have two or four bunks forward, a dining area, galley, refrigeration, and a fully enclosed toilet with a shower.

Over 40 feet?

A boat 40 feet and longer puts you in the lap of luxury. However, unless your boat is over 60 feet, don't plan on a transocean crossing.

> Some boats retain their **resale value** well while others lose it rapidly. For example, a top-of-the-line powerboat may lose only a small percentage of its value each year, while another boat may drop 25% the moment you drive it off the dealer's lot. Before buying a boat, it often pays to check the resale value of the boat to figure out how much you would get for your boat if you wanted to sell it. Resale value should always be considered when buying a boat, because you may probably want to sell it and get a larger boat in a few years.

What's the water like where you live? You don't need a 60-foot transocean cruiser if you are going to boat on a small river or lake. You will probably get more enjoyment from a smaller boat that allows you to moor up at a waterside café for lunch than from a large boat that needs a dinghy or launch service to get to the same café. If you plan on transiting the Intracoastal waterway, however, you will need a boat that can run all day at a slow speed and on which you can live aboard.

Do you want to boat on...small lakes and rivers?

Any boat will do for small lakes and rivers, but make sure that it has a shallow draft. Some rivers can be tricky to navigate. If you plan to travel down the Mississippi, buy a boat over 24 feet. In a smaller boat you will need to keep an eye on the weather and keep a Very High Frequency (VHF) radio tuned to the National Oceanic and Atmospheric Administration (NOAA) weather channel. At the first sign of bad weather, head for home.

Coastal waters or the Great Lakes?

Most boats can be used in coastal waters as long as you use them prudently. That means not going out of sight of land unless you have lots of experience. Larger boats can survive most bad weather, but you need to exercise caution if you go out of sight of land.

Open ocean?

If you plan to take your boat into the open ocean, get the largest boat possible and make sure you take lots of experienced crew with you. You will need to have the range (the distance the boat will go on one tank of fuel) to make it to a distant port. The boat must be well-constructed and able to handle anything the weather gods might throw at it.

Over 90% of the new and used production powerboats purchased today are made of fiberglass. Fiberglass is easily produced, easy to maintain, and lasts a long time. If you buy a used boat, it will most likely be made of fiberglass, although older hulls may be made of wood. Larger crafts are more likely to have a metal hull, either aluminum or steel.

Fiberglass boats

Fiberglass production boats are made on an assembly line with one line for the hull and all the equipment that goes inside and another line for the deck. As the boat nears the end of the production line, the hull and deck are joined together. This makes for a solid, watertight boat. All you have to do is buy the boat, paint the bottom, and polish the hull each year. When buying an older, used, fiberglass boat you need to be aware of damage. Always check the age of an older fiberglass boat. Older boats may be built with polyester resins, which, on boats that are kept in the water throughout the year, could cause osmotic blistering.

Wooden-hulled boats

If you are interested in restoration or want an inexpensive hull for your own use, a wooden boat may be for you. Many older Chris Crafts or Hackercrafts command high prices after a complete restoration. Typically, older boats are restoration projects that require a fair amount of work (and expense) to keep them in good trim. Plywood hulls are not often seen today, except in custom boats.

Metal boats

Steel and aluminum boats are not often found in smaller sizes. Typically, a steel boat will be in the 50- to 75-foot range unless it is a Dutch-built cruiser. Dutch shipbuilders have specialized in the fine art of building smaller steel craft. Resale value may plummet, however, if the new buyer does not appreciate European craftsmanship. Small steel boats also tend to be slow.

Aluminum hulls are about three times as expensive as steel and are usually reserved for large custom powerboats. In the smaller sizes, such as john boats, bass boats, and some skiffs, aluminum is a popular material. Typically, these small boats are machine shaped and pop-riveted rather than welded. Pontoon boats are also often made of aluminum and are usually used on freshwater lakes in the Midwest.

How will you get your boat to and from the water?

Where you keep your boat is very important. Many marinas and boat-yards with moorings have waiting lists, and it can take up to five years to get to the top of some lists. Likewise, waiting lists are common for liveaboard privileges. Typically, the larger the boat, the more difficult it is to find a space, so plan well in advance.

If you are forced to keep your boat in a marina, rather than on a trailer in your backyard, you may find that the marina costs break the bank or that launching the boat every time you want to use it is just too much of a chore.

Small boats (up to 15 feet) can be kept on a dolly or trailer and launched as required. Smaller boats, such as tenders or dinghies, can be carried on the roof rack of a car and simply wrestled into the water. Most boatyards have a dinghy dock where you can leave a small boat temporarily.

A trailerable boat can be kept in your driveway or a parking area with-out cost. Some homeowners' associations, however, may have restrictions on boat storage. Storage yards offer places for trailerable boats along with RVs and other spare vehicles. The cost of space in a storage yard or boatyard varies greatly, and you should check out the options for your trailerable boat. The drawback to keeping your boat on a trailer is that you must launch it every time you want to use it. This can get tedious if you use the boat every weekend. The advantage of having the boat on a trailer is that you can tow it to a new boating or fishing area quite easily.

Moorings

Your boat may require a mooring or marina slip if it is over 27 feet. In many parts of the country, there are mooring areas operated by clubs, government agencies, or private businesses. These moorings are rented and maintained by the operator. Sometimes there are restrictions on the size or weight of the boat permitted on a mooring. In any case, you will need transportation to get to your moored boat. Most boatyards have a shore boat that functions as a taxi for its members.

Marinas

The cost of a marina is typically more than the cost of a mooring. The advantage is that the boat is accessible simply by stepping aboard (for you and for thieves). Marina costs vary depending upon the location, age, facilities, and size of marina. Rent is usually charged by the foot on a monthly or seasonal basis. In most marinas, electrical power for onboard use and air conditioning, telephone installation, and possibly cable television are provided at extra charge. Water is usually free. If you are permitted to live on a boat in a marina, there is often a surcharge, although some enlightened marinas actually encourage liveaboards because their presence can serve as thief deterrence.

Privately owned docks

You may want to keep the boat at your home if you own waterfront property. But you should remember to include dock maintenance, seawall protection, and insurance costs in your budget. Think, too, about how you will protect your boat should bad weather or a storm arise.

For the majority of people, sole ownership makes the most sense, and is the simplest and easiest method of owning a boat.

Partnerships reduce the costs but typically last only about two to four years unless the partners are highly compatible. It's a good idea to ask yourself if you can afford the boat on your own if the partnership does not work out. Ideally, you should set your boat ownership up as a legal partnership to ensure that you do not become liable for your partner's accidents.

Payment becomes more complex for a partnership in that the bills for berth rent, insurance, and haulouts need to be timely with all partners contributing equally. Insurance companies and boatyards do not give individual billing and settlement checks to separate partners for their services. It's a good idea to set up a fund for replacement of gear, repairs, and insurance and have one of the partners responsible for the fund. To make a partnership function properly, you will have to use tact and diplomacy to work out an equitable plan for using and maintaining the boat.

Time-share or leasing

There are a lot of legal implications for group ownership that should be carefully considered. Time-share or leased boats have some of the same problems as partnerships. If you invest your money and aren't satisfied with limited access, rethink sole ownership in terms of value received. However, some group ownership schemes and chartering plans can qualify as tax breaks.

It is always a good idea to figure out exactly what you can do to reduce the **costs of ownership**. For example, you might paint the bottom and wax and polish the topsides in the spring. In the fall you may change the engine oil filters and check and replace the belts and hoses if needed. By performing this general maintenance yourself, you can reduce yard costs considerably. For example, boatyards charge almost $3,000 to winterize and cover a client's boat. If you can do this work yourself, you can put the money toward a larger boat.

How will you maintain your boat?

Your boat budget must consider the maintenance required to keep up a boat. Whether or not you do the work yourself, you should get the yard to look over your boat at the end of each season or once a year to find the kinds of problems that professionals are likely to spot. If you want to do it yourself, use at least one good book on boat maintenance so that you have some idea of the scope of possible problems.

If you keep a maintenance log and record anything that breaks or needs work, you are likely to discover most problems and get them fixed before they become major ones. The maintenance log will also help when you are ready to sell your boat. You will have a meticulous record of what work was done and when.

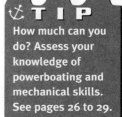

TIP

How much can you do? Assess your knowledge of powerboating and mechanical skills. See pages 26 to 29.

An annual haulout is essential for a boat. The cost includes taking the boat out of the water, power-washing it, chocking it onshore, painting it, and putting it back in the water. While it is out of the water, you should check underwater fittings and the zincs. Corrosion of the zincs usually indicates stray electrical currents, which means your wiring should be checked. Otherwise, replace the zincs, repaint the hull, and put it back in the water unless you intend to store the boat over the winter.

If you really want to keep your costs down and know how to repair **fiberglass boats**, look in the back of boatyards and marinas for older, discarded hulls. Quite often you can find a valuable hull that needs work for a few hundred dollars. Of course, you will have to put time and additional money into the project, but you will probably come out with a virtually new boat for a few thousand dollars.

Insurance

Insurance for smaller boats, such as those under 22 feet, is typically written as part of homeowner's insurance. Most large companies will include your boat based on a bill of sale and list of equipment. If you plan to trailer a boat, it's a good idea to check with your auto insurance agent first. For larger boats, you will need to deal with a specialist in marine insurance. You will need a marine survey to insure a used boat, and a survey may be needed for a new boat as well. In addition to paying the insurance premium, you will pay the cost of the survey. However, the survey then becomes your property, and may be used for other purposes, such as financing. Insurance premiums vary depending upon the value and age of the boat, building materials, and where you plan to use it. If you plan to go to foreign countries, investigate insurance costs carefully. Check the marina where you expect to keep your boat; it may require a special liability policy. A reasonable expense for domestic marine insurance is 1% to 2% of the value of your boat. Your insurance agent may also check your driving record to determine risk.

Financing

Banks and loan companies provide boat financing. Some companies specialize in marine loans. As indicated previously, if you finance a boat, you will need a current marine survey. The possible exception would be in the case of a brand-new boat. When you buy a boat, include electronics and other gear in the purchase price, so that the loan amount is sufficient. There are "blue books" for used boats. The loan officer will use the quoted price from the book and the marine survey to evaluate your loan. It is wise to check several sources for the best financing.

Taxes

Boats are subject to various taxes. Larger boats may be taxed as personal property or reassessed a use tax. Most states have some form of sales or excise tax levied by the state or county government. It is a common practice to purchase and register large boats out of state to avoid taxes. However, be aware that the practice of registering your boat in one place and using it in another could present problems.

I t isn't for nothing that boats have been described as holes in the water into which you throw money. There are indeed many costs associated with boat ownership. In colder climates boats need to be stored for the winter; they need to be insured both in and out of the water; and every time the boat goes into or out of the water, your boatyard will want to lighten your pocket. Following are some of the things you should consider:

Survey

Before you buy any powerboat over 18 feet long, get it surveyed. Most surveyors are competent professionals and can find things you may not have noticed. They will usually give you a list of work to be done either before or after you have purchased the boat. This list can be used to negotiate the price of the boat. In fact, a marine surveyor will probably save you more than the survey fee by enabling you to negotiate the purchase price.

Registration

Most states require boat owners to have a boat-driving license and registration for their boat, although this may not apply to small powerboats. Check your state's website or call the appropriate state department. In some states this is the Department of Motor Vehicles, in others the Taxation Department, while still others have the department under the Environmental Agency. Larger boats and boats that visit other countries are usually documented with the USCG. This is usually done through a documentation broker and is in lieu of local registration, but check your own situation carefully. Ask your yacht broker how to get your boat documented if it is over 40 feet or will go out of the country.

Storage

In locales where the water freezes, you will need a winter storage space. If you can keep a boat in your garage or backyard, the only cost may be the hardware for adapting space. Winter storage in a boatyard can be expensive. Whether you pay an annual fee for a mooring of $50 per foot per year or a monthly rental in a marina, you need to know the year-round cost of keeping the boat before you buy it. This means that you need to figure in winter storage costs.

Fuel

Fuel is an ongoing expense. Check your engine's fuel consumption by checking with the engine manufacturer and add it to your list of expenditures. Remember that two-stroke engines require oil as well. In general, gas engines use less fuel, but diesel fuel is less expensive.

> A major investment on a powerboat is the **engine(s)**. Look for engines that have been well maintained with low hours. If the engines are shot, ask yourself if the hull is worth the money you are paying for it. If it is, you can easily put in new engines.

What's your weather like?

Will the climate where you live let you use your boat year round? Most people north of the Mason-Dixon Line will answer "No." In this area people go boating from Memorial Day to Labor Day or late September and then haul out their boats. But if you keep your boat in the water later than Labor Day in the North, you can get some wonderful fall cruises. Boating on New York's Hudson River is a wonderful way to enjoy fall foliage.

South of the Mason-Dixon Line, the season is longer, but your boat will still have to be hauled out for a short period. In Florida and southern California, your boat can be kept in the water year-round.

At a minimum, you will spend (in the colder North) from $1,000 to $3,000, depending on boat size, per year in winter storage and decommissioning costs. If you pay a yard to do jobs such as winterizing your engines, draining water tanks, and covering your boat, these costs could easily rise to $10,000. In Florida, you will not have winter storage and decommissioning expenses, but you will have the cost of keeping your boat in the water, including an annual haulout and bottom painting.

Any boat that is kept in the water should be hauled out annually for inspection and bottom paint. Fiberglass boats need regular inspections and after 10 to 12 years may need painting. As previously mentioned, fiberglass boats that stay in the water year-round and were built prior to 1980 using polyester resins can develop blisters. This problem can be expensive to solve.

Engine maintenance is also essential and expensive. Outboard engines will need to be checked regularly. If they are used in saltwater they need to be flushed at the end of each season with fresh water, have the bottom unit oil changed, and the cylinders misted before being put away. Inboard engines require regular oil and filter changes. This should be done during the season if you run your engines hard and at the end of the season for moderate use.

At the end of the season, a competent mechanic should go over the engine to check hoses, wiring, and belts. The engine must be winterized by changing the crankcase oil and filters, draining the freshwater coolant, flushing the seawater coolant lines, and generally greasing and cleaning up the engine. Typically, this service at the beginning and end of each season puts the engine in good shape for the entire season. Other than running out of fuel, most well-maintained engines have few problems over the course of the season.

The Next Question: How Skilled Are You?

One way to evaluate your skills is to estimate the total number of hours you have been on a powerboat. If your experience is limited, there are various ways to increase it before you buy a boat. You can—and should—take Power Squadron courses, go out with more experienced boating friends, join your local boating club, or join the USCG Auxiliary. Going on the water requires that you observe the "rules of the road," know how to keep an eye on the weather, and avoid other boats. This information cannot be learned from a book. It needs to be experienced and practiced constantly. If you have spent less than a month on a boat, you should take a course or two before investing in a boat.

If you have had up to six months of boating experience, you can buy a boat, but you should probably get somebody with more experience to use it with you. Even then, you should file a float plan (see page 94) if you plan on any distance cruising or fishing. With a course or two under your belt, and a couple of years of boating experience behind you, you can pretty much buy whichever boat you want.

TIP
To gain experience before you buy your own boat, offer to crew on other people's boats.

While you can go to a dealer and buy a 50-mph boat with no experience, you should take advantage of any courses or guidance offered by the dealer. In the case of 80- to 90-mph boats such as the Wellcraft Scarab, the manufacturer offers a week-long, high-performance school to teach you how to handle the boat.

It is responsible boating to make sure you are as skilled as possible in handling your boat. You'll find that the more you know, the more confident you are and the more you and your family will enjoy being on the water.

Having said that, hours of practice are not the only indication of your expertise in powerboating. It's also important to learn boating skills while you are on board. If you have been a member of the crew, you followed instructions and learned to do specific things. Skills, if practiced regularly, build confidence in handling a powerboat. If the tasks have become easy and you anticipate the captain's orders, then your experience has begun to accumulate.

YOUR SKILLS/ABILITIES

Before you invest in a powerboat, ask yourself the following questions: Can you steer? Can you navigate? Can you bring the boat alongside? Do you know how to set up the dock lines and fenders? Can you anchor the boat properly?

While you may be daunted by the number of things there are to learn, taking a Power Squadron course can give you much-needed skills in the span of a few lessons. When you become the captain of your own boat, you'll continue to learn, but you'll also exercise the ultimate responsibility for the boat and the people aboard. Until you are confident that you can be in charge of the boat and the lives of the other people on the boat, take more experienced people along with you.

Boating Skills Checklist

Some specific boating skills that are important to have:

- Overboard rescue
- Steering
- Backing down or reversing
- Docking
- Anchoring
- Navigation

Overboard rescue If somebody falls off your boat, you need to be able to get him or her back aboard without running them down. Often the easiest way to do this is to stop your engines (turn them off so that the props do not revolve) upwind of the person and drift down to him or her. Once he or she is alongside the boat, you can haul him or her out of the water. If your boat has a high freeboard (the distance between the sea surface and the deck of your boat), you might want to invest in a ladder to help an involuntary swimmer get back aboard.

Steering Can you steer the boat in any direction and at any speed? Experienced boaters will tell you that steering downwind in heavy seas can be difficult. If you have problems steering the boat in any direction, the quickest way to make steering easier is to slow down.

Backing down or reversing On most single-screw boats, the stern will kick to port when you back it down. If you understand that this will happen, you can use the effect to help you dock the boat more easily. Twin-screw boats have contra-rotating props and generally back down in a straight line. However, you must beware of backing down at speed because you can put the transom underwater and swamp the boat.

Docking or picking up a mooring You need to be able to bring the boat alongside without damaging the dock, your boat, the boat next door, or your ego. That means that you need to know how to tie off the fenders and dock lines properly while watching all your crew to make sure they don't fall between the dock and the boat. You will also need to know how to pick up a mooring: always approach it uptide or upwind. That way the tide or wind will not carry you past the mooring buoy and you can adjust your speed to approach at dead slow.

Anchoring Imagine anchoring as using the parking brake on your car: you have stopped and need to keep your boat in the same position for a while. Before you use your anchor, make sure that the anchor line is tied to the anchor at one end and to a strong point on the boat at the other end. Many owners have tossed the anchor overboard only to find out that the other end was not tied to anything. Keep your fingers clear of the anchor when you toss it over and let it sit on the bottom before you attempt to secure it. Pages 104 to 107 tell you more about anchoring.

Navigation When you drive around on land, you stop at traffic lights, yield, or stop when you see the appropriate signs. Boats don't have traffic lights (except on some canals), but there are markers (buoys, posts, nuns, and cans) to tell you when you are in the main channel and other buoys that tell you to slow down or leave no wake. In addition to buoys, you need to learn about tides, charts, compasses, the Global Positioning System (GPS), radar, and the rules for passing another vessel. Just like drivers on land, mariners have rules for driving on water and you need to learn them. Navigation and rules of the road are taught in almost all courses.

YOUR SKILLS/ABILITIES

When you are out in a boat, you are on your own. If you can strip and repair an outboard, you have no worries. If you wonder which hand a screw driver goes in, make sure your Sea Tow subscription is paid up. Mechanical skills are not essential, but they will lower the cost of boat ownership. Each task that you can do for yourself will give you more confidence and independence. Sometimes a task may be too large for you to accomplish on your own, but the fact that you can diagnose a problem will make solving it easier.

Mechanical Skills Checklist

- Starting an outboard motor
- Repairing a pump
- Changing engine oil
- Checking a fan belt
- Surface preparation and varnishing
- Unclogging a head
- Using compasses

Starting an outboard motor Outboards now come with electronic fuel injection and various other sophisticated electronics that make it easy to start them and diagnose problems. However, in most cases repairing them is best left to an expert who has the right diagnostic tools and new circuit boards.

Repairing a pump There is a wide variety of pumps aboard larger boats. Pumps with diaphragms, impellors, or vanes are common. Learning to diagnose and repair pumps on your boat will save time and money. If you are unfamiliar with the types of pumps aboard your boat, get the mechanic at your local boatyard to show you the differences and how to repair them.

Changing engine oil This is a regular maintenance task with which you should be familiar. It can be messy, and, depending upon the type of engine you have, the oil sump drain plug may be difficult to reach.

Checking a fan belt Checking fan belt tension is relatively easy—you simply press on the belt. If it sags about $3/8$" to $5/8$", it's fine. More than that and you'll have to adjust the idler pulley to retension the belt. A build up of belt dust under the fan belt is a sign that things are misaligned.

Surface preparation and varnishing The charm of many boats is in the wooden trim used to finish the interior and exterior. This wood is referred to as brightwork. Learning to sand and varnish your brightwork requires patience but rewards you with a well-kept look to your boat. Many owners enjoy this task.

Unclogging a marine toilet Unclogging a head is an unpleasant task. If you make sure that the head is used properly, there is less likelihood of having to unclog it. However, if you have children with small toys, you will do it at least once. Taking apart and cleaning the head is a skill that will save you time and money, but this is a task you might want to spend money to have someone in a boatyard do.

Using compasses Proper knowledge and correct use of these instruments is essential for accurate navigation. They respond to magnetic influences and therefore can register incorrectly. You should hire an expert to swing your compass before you head to sea on your first trip. You should not place any ferrous objects near the compass.

Going it alone?

If you plan to boat alone, you are totally responsible for both yourself and your boat. You must be capable of handling the boat in all situations. Fishing alone, even on a small lake, requires extra vigilance because you can fall overboard and there will be no one to rescue you. You should file a float plan (let people know where you are going and when you'll be back) before setting out. Don't deviate from your plan, because if you get into trouble people may go looking for you in the wrong place. Carry a submersible portable VHF radio to call for help. Personal flotation should be worn all the time when you are onboard. Safety gear and electronic beacons are important, but you must still depend upon your ability to survive.

With others?

If you want to take family or friends on a special outing, be sure one of them is an experienced boater. If not, invite one. The safest course is to always have more than one experienced boater on board. Even so, plan to restrict your boating to protected waters and only tackle short distances. Before you leave the dock or launching pier, have everyone put on a lifejacket.

Taking children on a boat adds to your responsibility as captain. Young children should wear lifejackets onboard and even when they are on the docks around boats. Knowing how to swim is important, but an unconscious child cannot swim, so keep those lifejackets on. If you plan to cruise as a family, your children should learn about boats and become responsible crewmembers.

Many **people with disabilities** are able to participate in boating activities. Boats can be modified to increase mobility or limit the amount of physical strength required for particular tasks. A more difficult issue is the lack of balance or stability a disabled person might feel on a boat. Many disabled people can go on a day trip on a small boat with no problems. Overnight passages and spending a night on an anchor are more challenging. Racing presents more unpredictable situations than does cruising. Tasks that fall to the disabled person must be manageable regardless of weather

TIP
Taking an extra person on an overnight trip requires more than just another berth. It means more capacity for storage, food, water, and washing!

conditions or gear failure. Keep these eventualities in mind when you practice. If you have a disability or plan to boat regularly with someone who does, plan to modify the boat with swivel seats, ramps, and elevators. Shake-a-Leg, based in Newport, RI, is an organization for disabled boaters that can help with ideas.

Pets onboard?

Many people with cruising boats wouldn't think of boating without the family pet, but having a pet aboard takes careful planning. You need to think about food, water, and some toilet facility, even for day trips. For long trips, animals need to be trained to use litter boxes or a designated area. It is usually difficult for dogs to manage on a boat because the they don't have any way to grip the deck when the boat turns. Cats can adapt by holding on with their claws. Flotation for pets is advisable, particularly if there are heavy seas. Also bear in mind that getting a dog or other pet ashore is often difficult. Rules governing whether your animal may come ashore vary from place to place.

TIP

Keep your pets safe! Before you bring a pet aboard, get him his own personal PFD. The smallest pet vests also fit cats.

▲ A safety harness ensures that you know where your child is at all times aboard a boat.

You probably think that you will spend all your waking hours on your boat. Often that's true for the first few weeks, but then reality sets in. Chores still need to be done at home, and many other things eat into the time you can spend afloat. However, the good news is that most people use their boat a lot—every summer weekend and at least a week of their vacation time is not uncommon. Smaller boats get used more frequently, but not for vacations. Of course, you can figure out how much time your investment is worth to you, but most people look upon their time aboard as quality family time.

Live aboard

Of all the things you can do with a powerboat, living on one is probably the most satisfying and many are designed for that purpose. If you want to powerboat and live aboard at the same time, you will either have to get a big boat or do without some amenities. Most people who live aboard do so to simplify their lives.

Fishing boats

There are myriad boats out there. Many are adapted for special types of fishing. For example, bay skiffs and flat boats can operate in waters that are only a few inches deep and have a flat deck to enable the fisherman to walk around or pole the boat without tripping over gear. Bass boats are made for bass fishing and have a good turn of speed to get the fisherman to the grounds quickly.

Racing boats

Predicted log competition is possible with any kind of powerboat. In such competitions a boat owner must estimate the time it takes to go from one point to another and then go the distance in that time. The skill rests in knowing navigation, currents, and the characteristics of your boat.

Cruising

Trawler yacht cruising suggests a relaxed lifestyle where you are in charge. If you are happy with a pocket cruiser and trailering, you can enjoy cruising without huge initial costs or upkeep. Comfort, budget, and the number of people onboard will determine your boat selection and the kind of cruising you do.

As you expand your cruising horizons, you will spend more on amenities and a bigger boat that can accommodate them. Many older boatowners are investing in trawler-style yachts that have all the amenities of home. In these boats people cruise from Maine to Florida, up and down the Mississippi, and to many different places. Whatever the type of boating you want to do, there is a boat out there for you.

Are you a creature of comfort?

The comfort level you expect will be a big factor in deciding what type of boat to buy. If you expect to be dry, warm, and comfortable, sit on deck and read, use a toilet, take a shower, have hot meals and a comfortable bunk, you might buy a boat over 32 feet. Dinghies and open boats don't have toilets, so you may be faced with using a bucket, leaping over the side, or waiting until you get to land to obey the call of nature. In general, the larger the cruising boat, the greater the creature comforts.

TIP
If you know you will have small children on board, look for a boat with a deep cockpit, comfortable seating, shade, and a marine head.

If you decide to go ocean racing, your creature comforts will be minimal. You will need to wear flotation gear and maybe a harness. If you go on an offshore race, you may share a spartan bunk with someone else (known as hot-bunking), eat food directly from a hot can or pouch, and use a head protected only by a curtain.

An **annual budget** for your boat is a must. In general, you will spend about 4% to 8% of the purchase price a year on fuel. Maintenance for a new boat will be about 1% to 3%, and upgrading and maintaining a used or wooden boat will be about 10% to 15%. Interest will run about 2% to 4%. Estimate 2% to 4% for travel to and from your boat, and 2% on food and drinks. Assume that it will cost 3% to 5% of the boat's value just to repaint the topsides. New engines will cost several thousand dollars or about 40% to 60% of the boat's value, depending on the size and style of the engines.

If your boat does not come with an engine, you will have to decide what type to get. Gas engines are the least expensive, but they require safety precautions to make sure that the gasoline fumes don't blow up. Diesel engines are heavier, but have greater longevity, and the fuel is much less volatile.

On smaller boats between 25 to 34 feet, you have a choice of inboard or outboard engines. Inboard engines are set inside the hull and the prop shaft goes out of the bottom of the boat through a shaft log to the propeller. Some shaft logs do drip water because that's how they are lubricated. Others are the dripless type. An inboard engine requires a rudder to steer the boat; so the overall cost of an inboard installation is slightly higher than an outboard. Inboard engines are available from about 10 hp to several hundred hp.

Outboards hang off the back of the boat and are found on virtually all boats smaller than 25 feet. They have no shaft logs, and are turned to steer the boat. Outboards can be 4-cycle or 2-cycle. Four-cycle engines fire on alternate strokes and produce fewer emissions. They also have oil in the crankcase, whereas two-stroke engines fire on every stroke and the lubricating oil is mixed with the fuel oil.

Outboards have undergone tremendous changes in recent years as manufacturers have tried to conform to the California Air Resources Board (CARB) requirements. Typically, these requirements mean that emissions are reduced dramatically. The 2006 CARB requirements have even lower emissions and many of today's outboards already meet them. Outboards are available from 5 hp to about 300 hp, with one of the latest being Yamaha's 225 four-stroke that meets the 2006 CARB requirements.

Twin engines give the boat more maneuverability than does a single engine. With twin engines (inboard or outboard), the boat can be turned around in almost its own length. Twins also give more security in that most boats can get home on a single engine. Check this when you take a boat on a test drive (see Chapter 5). Single engines have the prop on the centerline and, because of the propeller torque, tend to turn the boat slightly. This problem is eliminated on a twin-engine installation because the props revolve in different directions.

How much time will you spend on maintenance?

How much time can you commit to maintaining your boat? Can you diagnose and repair major or minor problems? If you want to maintain your boat yourself, use at least one good book on boat maintenance, so that you have some idea of the scope of the problem. Whether or not you do the work yourself, you should get the yard to look over your boat at the end of each season or once per year to find the kind of problems that professionals are likely to know about.

In northern climes the boat will have to be hauled out at the end of the season, decommissioned, and made ready for winter. Over the winter, a major portion of the maintenance can be completed. But leaving all maintenance until you haul the boat out is not a good plan unless you have kept a meticulous record of what needs to be done and included it in the winter work list. If you do not have a record, you will most likely forget what should be done and have a problem next season. Also, it will be too cold to complete chores such as varnishing, polishing, and on-deck maintenance. Save these jobs for spring.

If you keep your boat in the water year-round, it will still have to be hauled out once a year. Before it comes out of the water, you should have a good idea of what work needs to be done and have any necessary supplies (paint, rollers, etc.) ready. You should also plan to do smaller chores while the boat is afloat. Varnishing, painting, and cleaning can easily be done on a sunny afternoon with the boat in the water. If you visit your boat regularly to clean, organize, replace parts, and paint or polish, you are more likely to discover most problems before they become major ones and your boat will remain in tip-top shape. If you only work on the boat the day you use it, chances are that you will be in a hurry, miss something important, or be rushed and fail to recognize the symptoms of a problem.

Keep a **maintenance log** of breakages, jobs that need doing, and anything else that should be done on the boat at periodic intervals. This log helps to demonstrate that the boat has been kept up properly when you are ready to sell it, and also ensures that you keep up with the work that needs doing.

CHAPTER 2

WINDOW SHOPPING

H aving addressed the questions in Chapter 1, you have a much better idea of what you want in a powerboat. You know what type of boat might fit your needs. Before you take any further steps, you should learn as much as you can about powerboats.

About Powerboats

There are so many different types of powerboats on the market that it is hard to know where to start. The principal groups are divided into categories, based on their speed. The categories are displacement hulls, transitional or semi-planing hulls, and planing hulls. There are also divisions inside each category based on the style of the boat. For example, a runabout is generally a small, fast (planing) boat, but older, slower runabouts may operate in the displacement mode.

The Displacement Mode

Boats that operate in the displacement mode tend to be slow, generally under 15 knots. However, the boat's actual speed is dependent upon a physical rule that says a displacement-hulled boat cannot travel faster than the square root of its waterline multiplied by 1.3. But a more realistic multiplier is 1.5 or 2. In other words, a 25-foot-waterline boat will go about 7.5 to 10 knots. You can push it a little harder, but unless the stern of the boat is shaped properly, the boat will be locked into wave crests at the bow and at the stern. Pushing harder creates a condition called squat and may cause the stern wave to break over the transom.

Boats in the displacement mode can be further divided into those that carry a heavy load, such as a trawler, and those that are long and narrow, such as a canoe or commuter-style boat. Trawler yachts have become very popular because they have a lot of space (in which all the comforts of home can be installed), while longer, leaner, commuter-style yachts give a smooth, easy ride at a reasonably high speed. Trawler yachts are boats such as the Nordhaven, Grand Banks, Albin, and others.

Semi-displacement Boats

Semi-displacement boats run at a moderately high speed but never actually get onto a plane (accelerate fast enough to generate hydrodynamic lift and skim across the top of the water).

Semi-displacement boats tend to trim (tip upwards) near the bow and to run at speeds up to about 20 knots, depending on the size of the boat. A planing boat may be cruised at semi-displacement speeds and accelerated to planing speeds if the owner needs to get home in a hurry. Examples of semi-planing boats are Viking yachts, some sportfishing types, some hard-chine trawler yachts, and a few of the older fishing boats.

Most powerboats that go fast are of the planing type. It is important to understand that any boat can be run at displacement speeds—that is, slowly—but not all boats can accelerate and get onto a plane. Ski-boats, high-speed fishing boats, sport boats, and deep-vee racing craft are in the planing category. Each boat has a specific use with handling and performance characteristics adapted for that use.

▲ **Water skiing: one of the many pleasures afforded by powerboating.**

SOME POWERBOATING TERMS

Deadrise: the angle of the slope of the hull bottom compared to the horizontal. Generally, deadrise angles are given as being at the stern, although designers may specify a deadrise angle near the bow.

Hard Chine: Where the vertical side of the hull meets the bottom at an abrupt angle.

Strakes: Sometimes called lifting strakes, these triangular structures are about 2" or 3" wide and run from forward to aft to help create additional lift on deep-vee hulls.

Round Bilge: A round-bottomed boat. Generally, round-bilge hulls are displacement hulls.

Planing: When the boat uses hydrodynamic lift to rise up out of the water and support about two-thirds of its weight from lift instead of displacement.

Displacement: Displacement is literally the weight of the boat. A boat that weighs 5,000 pounds displaces 5,000 pounds of water. Displacement can be taken as the dry weight of the hull (designers sometimes call this the light-ship condition). It can be calculated at half-load when all the crew, half the fuel, and water and provisions are onboard, or it can be taken at full-load. Generally, the weight published on the brochure is the design weight or design displacement. Some boats may be built considerably heavier than their design displacement.

Hole shot: Going from a standing start to full planing.

Specific types of powerboats have been developed to fill the various needs of boat users. In most cases, the hull has characteristics specific, but not limited, to that style of boat. For example, a runabout might have a cathedral hull similar to a Boston Whaler, or it might have a vee-hull similar to an Aquasport.

Runabouts

A runabout usually seats four to six people. Bowrider runabouts have additional seating in the bow accessed via a walk-though windshield. The runabout has no formal sleeping accommodation, but seats may fold down for sunning or napping. At about 18 to 20 feet, the enclosed part of the bow may feature a small cuddy cabin with enough space for a bunk or toilet, but not enough height for full headroom. While not luxurious, the cabin does offer shelter in wet weather and may make a good storage space for gear and electronics.

⚓ T I P
If you plan to scuba dive, make sure your boat has a swim platform in the stern.

Center consoles

The center-console boat is popular with anglers because it provides the maximum usable deck space for the boat's overall length. Seating is limited to one or two bench or swivel seats, so that fishing enthusiasts can handle rods or swing nets around the boat's entire perimeter. The lack of enclosed space, however, makes the boat undesirable for cruising. Center consoles range in size from less than 15 feet to about 35 feet.

Ski-boats

The speed of ski-boats is around 45 to 50 miles per hour to enable a skier to get up and to perform behind the boat. Ski-boats are designed to have a fairly flat bottom and to create a flat wake, to turn easily, and to tow a skier easily. They are not designed to head into big seas and high winds.

Wake-boarding boats

While they travel at about the same speed as ski-boats, wake-boarding boats are deliberately designed to generate a huge wake which will allow the boarder to make jumps and spins. They do this by having a fairly deep-veed hull, lots of weight aft to lower the stern, and specially shaped hull sides to entrain the wake so that it pops up aft of the hull. Some manufacturers offer a ski-boat that can be converted to a wake-boarding boat. The change is accomplished by adding a lot of water ballast in aft tanks, sinking the stern into the water, and generating a large stern wave.

Daycruisers

In the range of 20 to 25 feet, sportboats differ from daycruisers mainly in engine size and styling. However, the basic elements of their layouts are very similar. At this length, there is a very small cabin with sitting headroom in the bow. The day-cruiser cabin will probably have a V-berth, a portable head, and a small galley, consisting of a countertop stove, a basin, and a folding table.

Express and sedan cruisers

Express cruisers and sedan cruisers are differentiated by their accommodation layout. This is reflected in major differences in their hull and super-structure shapes. Express cruisers are one type of powerboat design, while sedan cruisers are another.

An express cruiser takes the basic sportboat configuration and enlarges it up to a length of 40 feet. The craft's foredeck is long and unobstructed. The control station, or bridge, is set well aft and raised a step above the cockpit.

A sedan or convertible cruiser puts the main interior space on the same level as the cockpit. The interior space is divided into two parts: a main saloon and the forward cabin below the foredeck. If there is a lower control station, it will be located at the forward end of the main cabin. These controls are often duplicated as a flybridge on a second level above the main cabin. The flybridge was originally intended as a platform to spot game fish. As length increases, it becomes possible to open up sleeping accommodations with an aft cabin below the level of the deck at the stern.

Inshore fishing boats

There is a large number of smaller, inshore fishing boats that look like their larger cousins and can usually travel just as quickly. However, they should not be taken too far offshore. To give plenty of room for anglers, these boats usually have a center console and wheel steering that drives a large outboard engine. Examples include Boston Whaler, Grady-White, Seacraft, and Albemarle.

Bass boats

Bass boats are slightly deeper and so can run in deeper water. They have a large engine to get them to the fishing grounds quickly, and usually use a trolling motor to move around slowly. Bass boats tend to have low deadrise and are not intended to be used in large seas and high winds.

Offshore fishing boats

Offshore fishing boats have a slightly higher deadrise angle at the stern. The bow also may have a fairly high deadrise angle to give a softer ride in the bigger seas that a fishing boat may encounter when it goes after larger fish. Smaller sportfishing boats up to about 20 feet can go up to 10 miles offshore. Larger sportfishing craft, such as a Blackwatch or a Luhrs, can go up to 60 miles offshore in search of tuna and sailfish. Examples of good sportfishing boats are Pursuit, Fountain, Wellcraft, and Bertram.

The major characteristics of sportfishing boats are the high freeboard forward that enables them to head into heavy seas and the low freeboard aft that enables a fisherman to reach to the water's surface and easily grab a large fish. This hull shape reaches its most extreme form in boats from Carolina, which can be used when onshore seas create very steep waves that require high bows with lots of flare.

Sportfishing boats can be convertibles that are rigged for fishing, or they can be true sportfishing boats with large cockpits and a fighting chair. Purpose-designed game-fishing boats usually have a tuna tower supporting a control station at maximum elevation for spotting fish and shoals.

Trawlers

A trawler is the name used for a comfortable cruiser that originally looked like an old-time trawler. Although trawler styles have changed, these boats generally include comfortable accommodations, single or twin engines, an enclosed bridge, a galley, and a saloon. Some trawlers cruise in the displacement or semi-displacement mode for long periods of time. These boats have been popular for traveling at 7 to 8 knots but may reach speeds of 16 to 18 knots. Slower speeds are ideal for waterways, where speeds are limited, and well-suited for long passages when fuel conservation becomes critical.

Tug yachts

Another popular genre is the tug yacht. These boats look like tugs with slightly higher freeboard and a cabin aft rather than a flat towing deck. These boats tend to operate in the displacement mode and have similar accommodations to a trawler-style yacht.

Catamarans

Catamarans offer the largest accommodations and space of any cruising boat. They can sleep a large number of people in separate cabins and usually have twin engines—one in each hull. The Transcat 48 (available from the Catamaran Company) provides three wide double berths in separate cabins with en suite toilets. On the bridge deck is a wide dining area and a large galley with a table that can seat everyone, including guests. This boat will power at about 26 knots and cruises at 22. Some sportfishing boats are catamarans, such as those from World Cats and Glacier Bay. They go just as fast as single-hulled boats, but offer a slightly more stable fishing platform with lower fuel consumption.

About Engines and Propellers

As mentioned in Chapter 1, there are several types of powering systems available for powerboats. Typically, the powering system is linked to the size and style of the boat. For example, runabouts and fishing boats under 25 feet tend to have outboards, while trawler yachts have inboard engines. High-performance boats may have inboard gas or diesel engines or up to five outboard engines mounted on the transom. A hydroplane, like the Miss Budweiser, may have a gas turbine engine. Some of the newer styles of boat, such as the Hinckley picnic boat, have water-jet drives to allow them to operate in shallow waters or waters where there are a lot of lobster pot warps.

No matter what the power system, the thrust from the engine is transmitted to the water via a propeller. The one exception to this rule is an ultra-high-performance, jet-engine-powered record-setting craft.

> If you're not sure how many hands will be on deck, get a boat that can be operated **single-handedly.** In a powerboat, this could mean a boat with twin engines and easy access fore and aft.

● ●

▲ **Propellers move a boat in the water using much the same principle as sails in the wind. Curved "foils" (the blades) create a pressure difference: low pressure on the forward surface and high on the aft. The foil shape is intended for forward rotation, which is one reason propellers are less efficient in reverse.**

Outboard motors are attached to the vessel's transom. They generally produce relatively high horsepower for their weight, and are somewhat more convenient to fit and service than inboard engines. Smaller outboards from 5 to 25 hp can be lifted off a boat's stern and stored separately, but larger outboards are bolted to the transom and are too heavy to remove regularly. Larger horsepower engine models up to 225 hp are suitable for use on boats into the 30-foot range.

Outboards are similar to your automobile's engine, except that the engine stands on end with the cylinders stacked one above the other. The camshaft points downward and drives a vertical shaft. This shaft goes via a gear case to a lower unit. At the lower unit, bevel gears turn the shaft 90 degrees and connect it to the propeller. Generally, the lower unit is bathed in oil that must be changed at the end of each season.

Steering is accomplished by turning the entire engine to change the direction of the propeller thrust. On most smaller boats, the engine is turned by a cable connected to the steering wheel. On larger boats the steering may be hydraulically connected.

Outboard engines work best when the propeller thrust is parallel to the surface of the water, so trim controls are often fitted on larger engines to adjust the angle of prop thrust. Other boats have engines mounted on platforms aft of the hull to help keep the prop thrust horizontal.

Engine trim controls

An outboard can be trimmed—that is, its angle can be adjusted to keep the prop shaft and prop thrust parallel to the sea surface. This adjustment allows the outboard to be raised out of the water to keep it clean when the boat is not in use.

Trim tabs

Some boats have trim tabs mounted on the transom to control the trim angle of the boat. As the boat accelerates onto a plane, the bow lifts up into the air. By lowering the trim tab, water is deflected downwards at the stern and the bow is lowered. However, cranking in too much trim tab can slow the boat down and make it more difficult to get the boat on a plane.

The latest in outboard engines

If you have ever seen an old two-cycle outboard start up, you will have noticed the cloud of blue smoke emitted by the engine as it warms up. Today, that cloud of smoke, which contained all manner of pollutants, has almost disappeared. Limiting emissions has become highly important, as evidenced by the claims of many outboard manufacturers that they meet the 2006 CARB (California Air Resources Board) emissions requirements. The use of electronics in engines allows manufacturers to monitor emissions, which in turn leads to virtually every new engine being able to meet emissions requirements for the 2001 model year. Suzuki has a new four-stroke, fuel-injected, 115 hp outboard that meets 2006 EPA standards as well as the 2008, ultra-low 3-star CARB guidelines. This engine is 80 pounds lighter than a comparable engine and has a 2.59 to 1.00 reduction gear that allows it to swing a larger prop with increased pitch. One drawback: the engine is so quiet that many users forget that it is running and try to start it again. Among larger engines, the 135 hp Mercury, the OMC 250 with Ficht fuel-injection, and the Yamaha 225, all meet or exceed the 2006 EPA emissions standards.

▲ An inboard-outboard's "outdrive" or "lower unit" permits the coupling of a powerful inboard engine with a steerable and trimmable propeller shaft. This configuration has become popular for powerboats from 18 to 28 feet.

Inboard engines are installed entirely within the hull and must drive the propeller through the shaft log, which keeps water from entering where the propeller shaft passes through the hull. Many inboard engines are developed from automobile engine blocks. Typically, an inboard engine slopes slightly downward to give the prop some clearance and stop it from hitting the hull. The nearer the propeller is to the horizontal, the better the engine thrust is transmitted to the water. Steeply tilted engines may suffer from lack of lubricating oil in the highest cylinders, which can lead to engine failure.

Ideally, prop shafts should be supported every few feet with either a bearing or a pillow block to prevent them from whipping. The propeller shaft goes through the hull at the shaft log or one of the other styles of stern gland. Outside the hull, the shaft is supported by a strut immediately in front of the propeller. Inside the strut is a cutlass bearing. On a used boat this bearing should not show signs of wear. A worn cutlass bearing is usually a good indication that the engine is misaligned.

Gas or diesel: which is best?

There is an ongoing debate about inboard engines. Some users prefer lighter, faster, gas-fueled engines, while others prefer heavier, slightly noisier, slower-to-react diesel engines. The pros and cons are simple. Gas engines are less expensive initially, so the boat is cheaper to buy. Gas engines use fuel that can be purchased anywhere. Gas engines are lighter, so the boat can go faster; and, finally, when you accelerate, a gas engine reacts quickly and the boat moves out. However, a big problem with a gas engine is that fumes from the fuel can fill the boat and may eventually ignite. The explosion of a gasoline-fueled boat will literally blow the boat to pieces.

Diesel engines are heavier than gas engines. This is because the fuel is compressed to get it to ignite rather than being sparked as in a gas engine. The compression forces require a more strongly built engine. Because the engines are slightly heavier, the boat generally does not go as fast as a gas-powered sister ship. Diesel fuel is not volatile like gasoline, but diesel engines are slightly slower to react than gas engines. With turbocharging and after cooling, diesels are now getting closer to the reaction time of gas engines. Diesels also tend to last longer than gas engines because they are more heavily built.

Electronic monitoring of engines

E lectronic monitoring of engine performance started when Detroit Diesel came out with its DDEC system, and it hasn't ended yet. Black boxes are linked to virtually every piece of onboard equipment to provide a complete picture of what is happening to a boat.

The SmartCraft system from Mercury Marine allows Mercury engines to be linked to an Electronic Control Module (ECM) that also takes input from many of the other onboard systems, such as the bilge pump, the fuel tank, and the transmission oil. However, the Mercury system can only be used by Mercury engines, although other ECM equipment with approved sensors can be linked to the black box. In addition to the ECM, Mercury's Optimax engines feature the Guardian system. This system uses the ECM to monitor the engines and warn the operator before an engine-damaging event can occur. It also tells the operator how to correct the problem. By plugging in a computer to the ECM, a mechanic can diagnose problems in minutes and make the appropriate corrections.

Teleflex, on the other hand, has the "Magic Bus." This is an open-architecture system that allows the user to link virtually anything to anything else. With the Magic Bus system, you can link engine instruments, autopilot, wind instruments, radar, bilge pumps, and other electronic equipment to the system to get virtually seamless integration.

Magic Bus and the SmartCraft system are both available to fit the new National Marine Electronic Association (NMEA) 2000 standard. The NMEA 2000 standard allows information from all over the boat to be sent to other onboard equipment, a central onboard computer, or even to a shore-side diagnostic platform. In a few years, the NMEA 2000 standard will be the only one in use aboard boats. It allows electronic equipment and instruments to be added and removed simply by plugging them in or unplugging them. You will be soon able to "plug and play" electronics, engine monitoring systems, navigation systems, the stereo, TV, and the autopilot on a boat as easily as you use your home computer.

Propellers

Propellers should be thought of as pumps that accelerate a circular cylinder of water aft to push the boat along. In nautical slang, propellers are also sometimes known as "props" or "wheels." Propellers are usually classed by the number of blades, their direction of rotation, their diameter, and their pitch. For example, a three-blade, right-hand, 13" x 19" turns clockwise (in forward gear), is 13 inches in diameter, and theoretically travels forward, or has a pitch of, 19 inches in one rotation. However, because water is a fluid and the boat is moving forward, the prop does not actually travel 19 inches during one revolution. The distance between the prop's actual travel and its pitch is called its efficiency.

▲ The adjustable-pitch propeller answers the need for greater efficiency through a wide range of speeds.

Collecting Boat Information

You will want to collect as much information as possible about any boats that are of interest to you. You can find material in a number of places, such as articles and advertisements in magazines, on the Internet, from dealerships, and boat shows. Some periodicals you might want to check out in your local library include *Power and Motor Yacht*, *Go Boating*, *Powerboats*, *Motor Boating* and *Soundings*.

The Internet has so much information that a good search engine can save you lots of time and running around. Most major powerboat makers have their own websites where you can look for more specific information about boats that interest you. There are also websites that provide general information about powerboats, such as www.allaboutboats.com and www.powerboats.com. You can also check out www.Boattest.com, a site that has factual reviews of boats online. Print out any pages you think you might want to refer to later. That way, you'll have a home library for ready reference.

If you know you're interested in a used boat, there are a number of sites that can make your search easier. The three largest sites are:

► www.traderonline.com

► www.yachtworld.com

► www.soundingsonline.com

At each site, you can search powerboat databases by boat length, manufacturer, price, or year built. For comparing boat prices, check out the NADA Appraisal Guide site at www.nadaguides.com. This site offers pricing information from the guide itself.

If you want to see what's available in your area, go to the website of your local newspaper, where you can access the classified section. Depending on the newspaper, the classifieds may be updated every day or every week.

B oat shows provide most buyers with the best opportunities to make comparative decisions. Even if you are convinced that you will be buying a used boat, consider attending boat shows. You will derive greater benefit from any boat show by doing a little "homework" beforehand.

Start with the brochure:

► Look at the numbers first to get a feel for the boat. Is it the right length overall? The longer the waterline, the faster the boat.

► Is the beam adequate?

► Are the bunks carried into the ends of the boat (where the motion of the boat will be exaggerated)?

► Is the galley suitable for your type of cooking?

► Is the engine adequate? Remember: adding extras like a larger alternator or a bilge pump robs the engine of 3 to 5 hp.

► What type of keel is it? A deep keel keeps you out of a lot of harbors; a shallow keel may reduce stability.

After you have narrowed your list to six or eight boats, go to a boat show. If your schedule permits, choose a day when attendance is low. Usually, the first "Red Carpet" days have the lowest attendance. Bring a notebook, a tape measure, and a camera. Take time and carefully go over each boat that interests you.

Hop aboard and look the boat over. Use your tape measure, because appearances can be deceiving. Check the length of the berths (they should be at least 6 feet 4 inches); check the widths (at least 28 inches). Check the dining table size and the table seating. Do you have enough seats for your cruising party? Do you have enough berths?

If you narrow it down to one or two boats, ask to make arrangements for a trial voyage. While you spend a lot of time at a show looking at boats, don't forget that equipment matters, too. Equipment manufacturers may also be represented at the show, so visit them, too, and see whether they have newer or better equipment that may not be shown on the boats. If you come away feeling overwhelmed, you're not alone. Remember that your opinions may change quickly as you gain some experience, so don't plan to make a purchase decision based solely on a boat show encounter.

By now, you may be able to narrow your choices down considerably. When you begin shopping, you can limit the number of boats you see to 10 instead of 30. Or, if you prefer not to run from dealership to dealership, you can shop by phone. A trained salesperson should be able to convey quite a bit of information in a relatively short period of time.

Here are some of the questions you will want to ask:

► Which models (of daycruisers, or runabouts, or fishing boats, etc.) do you have in stock?

► What options does the boat have?

► What kind of motor does it have?

► What is the boat's construction?

► How much do the boat and motor cost? Don't assume the first price you're given over the phone, or even in person, is final. Like buying a new car, it can take a lot of back and forth to make a deal.

► What is the ordinary wear and tear on the boat?

► How does the boat handle in rough water?

► How does it compare to other boats you've been looking at?

► What's the standard hull warranty? The motor warranty?

> **TIP**
>
> A new boat has a comprehensive manufacturer's warranty covering at least the first year. Make sure you get a written copy of the warranty—and read it!

After you've looked at a number of ads, you'll be ready to go out and look at some boats yourself. Decide on the manufacturer or style of boat you want before going to a broker or before you get into the car. Seeing everything listed is exhausting and ultimately a waste of time. You might want to talk to the seller before you actually go see the boat. Whether in person or on the phone, you'll want to encourage the boat owner to talk. The more you find out about the boat and the owner's experiences with it, the better able you'll be to decide whether to buy.

Here are some of the initial questions you'll want to ask the seller:

► Why are you selling the boat?

► How old is the boat? How long have you owned it?

► How long has the boat been on the market? Are you in the process of negotiating with anyone else?

► How much are you selling the boat for? Are you flexible on the price? How did you determine that price?

► What are the boat's major strengths? Major weaknesses?

► What kind of repair work have you done?

► Do you have the maintenance records?

If you are seriously interested in the boat, you should do a thorough inspection of it before proceeding any further. (See Chapter 5 for what to look for during an inspection and whether to hire a marine surveyor.) You might want to come prepared to do your own inspection the first time you see a boat. Even if you have not scheduled enough time for a full inspection, you will certainly want to bring your crew with you on your initial trip. Chances are that you'll be making your decision with your boating partner or family, and you'll want their opinion up front.

Now you are zeroing in on the boat of your choice. If you are looking for a used boat, you can continue to look at each boat on your own or you can go to a yacht broker. In general, yacht brokers can search more listings, get a feel for more boats, and give you an idea of the type of boat that will appeal to your price and appetite much faster than you can find it on your own. Most brokers subscribe to a multiple-listing database that shows boats that may not be advertised. Consequently, there is no need to go to three or four brokers, because one good one can do everything any other broker can. A broker who knows your tastes and has an idea of your purse may call to tell you that he or she has just the boat for you.

Brokers can save you lots of work, as they generally inspect the boats they have to sell and list information about each boat on their listing service. For example, a broker in Maine may find just the boat for you in North Carolina. Rather than have you hop on a plane or drive for many hours to view the boat, the Maine broker will call the listing broker in North Carolina and ask about the boat's condition and inventory. This information will get relayed to you.

When you are buying a boat, the broker works for you. He or she should have your goals and aims in sight and will communicate your offering price to the selling broker. This often means that your broker will contact the listing broker. The two brokers will handle all the paperwork and some will document or register the boat for you. All you do is sign on the dotted line and go get your boat.

When you are selling a boat, the broker works for you. He or she screens all bids and will usually only submit serious offers to you, cutting out nonsensical offers.

For this service, there is a brokerage fee that will usually be around 10% of the boat's price. This fee is often split equally between the broker of the buyer and of the seller, and then split again between the broker and the company that he or she is working for. Consequently, brokers may see as little as 2.5% of the boat's price for all the work they put in.

CHAPTER 3

WHAT CAN YOU AFFORD?

Having done as much research as you can on powerboats, you have a good idea what you want out of a boat. You know what kind of boat you're interested in. Now comes the crucial question: **What can you afford?**

The Cost of a Powerboat

Multi-millionaire J.P. Morgan once said about buying a boat, "If you have to ask how much it costs, you can't afford it." But most of us aren't so privileged. We need to know exactly how much we're going to spend and whether we can (or should) do it.

As with other important purchases in life, when buying a boat, you need to consider not only your initial cost, but also how much you will spend on a monthly basis. It's also important to remember that while a boat is an investment, it rarely sells for more than the price you paid for it. There are exceptions to this rule, but generally, they are high quality, in-demand boats. Most boats depreciate, just like cars. In general, the lower the quality of construction, the more the boat is likely to depreciate.

As most people tend to overestimate their purchasing power, it is better to start with a smaller boat and, as your skills and seamanship increase, move up to a bigger boat. Begin by being frugal, knowing that you can trade up later.

Price

Prices of new boats vary depending on the quality of construction, the boat's displacement (in general, the greater the displacement, the more expensive the boat is), the size and power of the engine, the equipment on board, and many other factors. As a first-time buyer, take the time to find out from other boat owners which boats have a good reputation and which ones are just, well...blah. When it comes time to resell your boat, you'll be pleased that you picked the one with quality construction.
It will sell more quickly and for more money.

Boats of comparable quality can be compared in terms of cost per pound of displacement. For example, suppose a boat costs $20,000 and weighs 4,000 pounds. It costs $5.00 per pound. Of course, when you make this type of comparison, you need to make sure you are comparing apples with apples. A boat that comes with a basic engine package, instruments, lifejackets, fenders, bottom paint, and is ready to go into the water will cost more per pound than a boat in which the engines and equipment are optional extras.

Usually, you can negotiate with the seller of a new or used boat. A new-boat dealer often has some flexibility in agreeing to a price, especially if the economy is in a downturn. Both parties compromise a little, and everyone can feel good about the final transaction. Used boats are always subject to negotiation. Owners often accept offers lower than the asking price.

> The world is full of small boats sitting on trailers with a **"For Sale"** sign on them. Don't be afraid to make an offer on a boat that suits your boating style. When making a bid, start by offering about 15% to 20% less than the asking price and be prepared to negotiate. This means that if you have $5,000 to spend you, can look at boats that are priced around $6,000 or slightly more.

Quality

It is usually apparent, when examining two boats of the same length, why one is more expensive than the other. One boat may have hand-made cherrywood furniture, while another has plastic laminate. One might have a 350-horsepower, aftercooled, turbocharged diesel engine, while another has a naturally aspirated gas engine. You do get what you pay for, at least when it comes to new boats.

Knowing what represents quality in a boat is something you learn after spending some time aboard boats. If you are buying your first boat, take the time to read magazine articles that describe the interiors of boats. Ask friends, boatyard managers, and boatowners what they think gives a boat quality. Go to boat shows and go aboard as many boats as you possibly can. Take pictures, make sketches, collect brochures, and above all, ask questions. Sales professionals are always willing to answer questions.

Find out what the highest-quality boat at a boat show is and take a walk through it. Look at the quality of the furniture (sometimes called joinerwork). Look at the material used for countertops. Top-of-the-line boats may have granite or marble, moderate-level boats may have Corian, rather than the plastic laminate found in less expensive boats. The least expensive boats often have bare fiberglass countertops. Bare plywood edges on locker doors set in a recessed fiberglass locker are at the lowest level of construction. Doors with rounded corners and trimmed with wood or with wood-laminate indicate a much higher level of construction.

Payments and Interest

Cash is best, but most people finance their boats for up to 15 years. Financing makes it possible to enjoy your boat while you are paying for it. It also means that, with interest, you can eventually end up paying almost twice the principal. The easiest way to estimate five-year payments at 8% to 10% interest is by multiplying the number of thousands by 20 and dividing by 1,000—that is, a $5,000 boat will have payments of around $100, a $10,000 boat will run about $200, and a $20,000 boat will cost around $400 per month.

If you don't know the prevailing interest rate, call a bank to find out. Then figure out how much you can pay as a down payment. These two figures should give you a good idea of how much you can pay for a boat. Another way to find this information is to go to a boating or banking website and look at their interest tables. Many financial and boating websites have a loan calculator where you input the amount of the loan, the interest rate, and the length of the loan, and you are given the monthly payment.

PAYMENTS ON A $50,000 BOAT AT 10% INTEREST		
Term	Monthly payment	Interest over full term
60 months	$1,062.35	$13,741.00
120 months	$660.75	$29,290.00
180 months	$537.30	$46,714.00

Depreciation

Depending on the quality of the boat you purchase, its value could drop the first time you use it. Some of the more expensive boats, such as a half-million-dollar Hinckley Picnic Boat, will almost hold their cost, and in times of high demand or high inflation may sell for more than the purchase price. But generally boat prices drop. Higher-quality boats depreciate less than low-quality boats. To find out approximately how much your boat will be worth in three years, compare prices of three-year-old boats when new to their price today. For example, a three-year-old-boat that was bought for $60,000 may be worth $45,000 today, which is a drop of 25%. In general—and there are no hard and fast rules—you could expect a boat by the same manufacturer to drop a similar amount. However, a superbly maintained boat with a lot of extras may only drop in price 10%, whereas a boat that has not been maintained and is scraped or damaged may drop 40%.

Depreciation is very useful when you are buying a used boat, but discouraging when you are paying off a 15-year loan. Just remember—the ultimate value of a boat lies in the enjoyment you get out of it, not the money you put into it. By checking resale values before you buy a boat, you will end up getting a better deal and preserving more of your money. By taking meticulous care of your boat over the period of your ownership, you can also preserve more of your capital investment.

Marine Mortgage

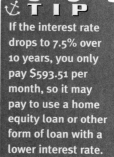

TIP

If the interest rate drops to 7.5% over 10 years, you only pay $593.51 per month, so it may pay to use a home equity loan or other form of loan with a lower interest rate.

The majority of us will have to seek financing when we buy a boat. Once an offer to buy the boat has been accepted, the buyer needs to secure financing. At that point, he or she will find a bank or lender and negotiate the down payment and interest rate as well as the appropriate collateral.

The next obstacle is the establishment of clear title and non-encumbrance liens, mortgages, etc. Usually a broker will help you determine this or point you to a person who can. In most cases this is slightly more difficult in the boat market than in the automobile market. The net result is that boat loans require a greater down payment on the borrower's part and often additional collateral in the form of a home mortgage. Typically, a marine mortgage carries with it the whole range of rights and obligations that accompany any property mortgage.

Insurance

Just as with automobile loans, the lender of a marine mortgage will require proof of insurance coverage. The cost of insurance can vary widely, depending on the class of boat and where it is insured. Rates increase, for instance, in areas prone to hurricanes and tropical storms. But rates differ from company to company as well. It is best to shop around before settling on any one insurance company, or you may end up paying twice as much as you need to. You can expect at least a 1% deductible ($1,000 on a $100,000 boat), so although insurance will pay for major repairs, it won't cover all the minor damages your boat will suffer in the course of a year.

Actually owning a boat involves a lot more than just monthly loan payments. First, there are the overhead costs, like mooring or storage fees, insurance, and fuel. Moorage prices differ so much from area to area that it is impossible to estimate here what you might have to pay. Even in the same town, costs may range from as little as $6 a month per foot for a mooring to $30 a month per foot for a slip in a popular marina. When you factor in electricity and water, the cost of a marina may be even higher. It is crucial that you investigate where you will keep your boat before you buy it so that you can keep the cost within your budget.

You may discover that the marina you had planned on is far too expensive or that it has a waiting list of a few years. If you leave your boat on a mooring you will need to factor in the additional cost of using a launch to get to it. This can be another $50 to $250 per season. If, on the other hand, you decide to trailer your boat, you will need to buy a trailer and perhaps rent a storage facility to store it in, or store it in your yard. Again, prices will vary from region to region. Whatever your combination of storage and access will be, try to get a sense of what it will cost before you buy the boat. (If you plan to buy a truck to haul your trailer around, factor in the cost of that, too!)

Monthly insurance will cost at least $30 to $50; monthly repair costs for disposables, such as touch-up paint, varnishes, polishes, and spare parts, may run as high as $100. Then there's the cost of fuel. Oil and gas prices fluctuate, and this must be factored in. If you run out of fuel, you will need a tow back to harbor. The U.S. Coast Guard no longer gives provides towing, but will direct you to a commercial operator who may charge up to $300 if you are not a member of that operator's plan.

Fitting Out

It is rare that a new boat comes equipped with enough fenders, dock lines, ground tackle, and spare parts. You will need to buy these as well as the necessary safety equipment to commission the boat for insurance purposes, such as personal flotation devices, tool sets, fire extinguishers, first aid kits, flares, anchors, and anchor lines. Pick up a catalog from your local marine chandlery or hardware store and estimate prices accurately before you buy.

Brokers

Since buying a used boat is legally complex, many buyers and sellers seek the help of a broker. When you're buying a used boat, it is crucial to find the right broker. While there are brokerage associations that endorse brokers, brokers tend to do business according to local custom. Their fees vary, and the range of service that they provide can vary a great deal, too.

Usually, a broker will make an agreement with a seller. Once the agreement is signed, the broker begins to advertise and show the boat. When the buyer and seller arrive at an agreeable price and terms, usually by working through the broker, then an agreement to purchase is drawn up based on a fairly standardized document.

An important aspect of this agreement to purchase is that a future closing date is specified. In the intervening time, the buyer can investigate title and search for state registered bills of sale, chattel mortgages, and other claims, such as sales tax, that may exist on the boat.

Some brokers will agree to list a boat non-exclusively and will advertise it on a multiple-listing service. These services can be a great advantage to the buyer, to whom boats will be available not just locally, but nationally and worldwide, using the Internet. If you have a broker who listens to your needs, you have a very good chance of finding just the right boat for you. It may be true that some brokers will try to push a boat you're not very interested in, but generally, those who want to attract more business will do their best to accommodate you. If you are a first-time powerboat buyer, finding an experienced broker might be the wisest thing you can do.

> After you own a boat you might want to join an organization such as **Boat/US** to take advantage of their discounts, towing service, insurance, and financing packages.

CHAPTER 4

BUYING A USED BOAT

W hen you are buying a new boat, the manufacturer will usually build the boat to recognized standards. But when you buy a used boat, you need to know what to look for to determine whether the boat is in good condition.

First Impressions: Trust Them

When you inspect a used boat for the first time, you'll notice many things. The boat may be in good condition, it may be moderately maintained and in easily upgraded condition, or it may be a disaster—what boatyards call a "project boat."

A boat in top-notch condition will be clean, shiny, well polished, and have the look of efficiency. It will smell of cleaners, paint, and varnish. The engine compartment may smell faintly of oil, possibly paint, and the bilge will be clean. The owner has kept the boat in good shape to maximize its resale value.

> **⚓ T I P**
> Before you take a look at a used boat, visit one of the many sites on the Web and find out more about the type of boat that you want to buy.

A boat in not-so-hot condition may look a little like a run-down motel. Telltale signs include mildew and mold on the deck and hull, dirt and trash accumulation in corners and around drains, and rust streaks running down the deck or hull. When you go inside, you may smell bad plumbing or dirty bilges. Running your hands inside lockers and under shelves, you might feel moisture from leaks or condensation. When looking at such a boat, try to judge whether the condition is merely superficial. Maybe a good cleaning and a little paint will get the boat "shipshape." If this is so, you may be able to make a low offer and get a good boat for less than the cost of a pristine boat. Be wary though—real problems could be lurking under the grime.

A project boat will be in worse shape. The hull may have scrapes and dents, the woodwork will be gray and uncared for. If the boat has been standing under trees, the hull may be full of leaves and dirt. If you are going to buy a project boat, you need to look beyond the mess and at the structure. If the structure is sound, estimate whether or not you can restore the boat for less than the cost of another used boat.

If you decide that you like restoration and repair projects, try to assess your skill and your available time. Can you complete the project? If you cannot, can you afford to hire someone to help you or to finish the project for you? Answer these questions honestly before attempting to restore or repair a used boat.

A smaller boat, generally under 20 feet, or one in which your investment is small, usually does not warrant the cost of a survey and it will be left to you to examine your potential purchase very carefully to make sure there are no problems. Larger boats are usually surveyed, but you can do some preliminary checking yourself. On the next page is a specific checklist of things to inspect. Some of the items listed won't apply to a small boat. However, this list will help you evaluate the whole range of powerboats, even those with complex systems. As you examine the boat, maintain your objectivity and make notes. If you find problems that you can't fix or ignore, check with a surveyor or move on to another boat. Don't settle for the first boat you see just because you have your heart set on buying a boat. Examine several boats before you choose the one for you.

> **TIP**
>
> A must-have used boat guide is the BUC Used Boat Price Guide, published by BUC Information Services. Also known as the "blue book," it has a website at www.buc.com.

Collect Your Tools

You will need a few simple tools to inspect a boat. Take along a ruler, bronze wool, a small mirror, a flashlight, a magnifying glass, a pencil and notepad, and a camera. Digital cameras are handy if you have to send information to a manufacturer to make sure you are getting the correct replacement part. The ruler turned onto its edge will indicate if surfaces aren't flat. Bronze wool will wipe away rust so that you can examine any steering swages for cracks. Never use steel wool; it leaves tiny shards of steel that will eventually rust and leave marks. It often takes a magnifying glass to see hairline cracks in the hull or deck. A small mirror is useful for looking behind hoses, engines, and other hard-to-see places. A flashlight is great for looking into bilges and lockers. A rag keeps your hands clean if you get into grease and oil. You'll need a pencil and notepad for your notes.

Armed with your tools and the following checklist, allow sufficient time to inspect the boat carefully. It is important to see a boat in the water and out of the water. If you do all the in-the-water assessment and feel certain you are interested in the boat, then you will need to arrange to see it out of the water. If you think this is a potential purchase, you may want to wait until you've looked at several boats and then have the best one hauled out.

IN-THE-WATER CHECKLIST

This list should give you an idea of what to look for. Some solutions are proposed to give you an idea of the amount of work required to fix them.

Problem/Implication/Solution

1. **The boat lists (leans) to either side.** Check to see if the list is caused by incorrectly-stowed gear. If the boat leans to one side, it could be that equipment is improperly installed. If the equipment is installed properly...well, the boat might just lean.

2. **There are broken strands on the steering cables.** If you find broken strands, the cables need replacement. This is usually an inexpensive job.

3. **The cable steering is stiff.** It may just need lubrication. If it binds, the cable may be bent too tightly.

4. **The stanchions and pulpits do not line up on both sides.** This could be poor installation or damage caused by poor docking technique.

5. **The deck is uneven and there are pockets of dirt.** Uneven decks may be signs of damage and should be looked at by a professional. Note that fiberglass decks can flex and still be strong enough. However, most boat owners do not like decks that flex, so they are usually built with more stiffness than required.

6. **Cracks in the fiberglass.** These could be cosmetic or structural. Determine whether the crack goes right through the laminate or just through the gel coat. Cracks in the laminate are serious, and cracks in the gel coat may let water into the core material and thus should be checked for rot. Have a surveyor or the boatyard help to determine the type and severity of any cracks you find.

Steering Problems

7. **The view from the helm is obstructed.** You should also check to see that you can view all parts of the deck. That way, people on deck can be watched to ensure they don't fall off.

8. **The rudder feels loose and sloppy.** This could be a sign of worn bearings or cables, or bad installation. Have your yard or surveyor check it carefully.

he engine gear and throttle levers are stiff. This is usually caused by nadequate lubrication in the cable or a cable that turns too sharply and inds. Either get the yard to lubricate it or install new cables.

There are bubbles in the compass. Bubbles are caused by leaving the cover off the compass on a hot day. This causes the alcohol to expand out through the over-pressure vent. It does no harm to the compass, but makes it difficult to read.

The instruments are hard to see or read. Instruments that you need to ead regularly should be in front of you. Switches and instruments that you do not need to read can be to one side or the other.

Foredeck and Anchoring Gear Checks

Look for sturdy anchoring gear appropriate to the size and weight of the boat.

Make sure the bow is fitted with a proper sized anchor roller.

Make sure the inboard end of the anchor rode is secured to a structural part of the vessel. Many anchors have been tossed over the side without being tied on.

Operate the anchor windlass—raise and lower it.

Check that bowrails and pulpits are firmly through-bolted.

Check that the bow chocks and cleats are adequate for the size of the boat.

Make sure that the bow lights work.

Check to see that the forward hatch does not leak.

Electrical System Check

Check that the navigation lights work.

Make sure that the steaming light or lights operate.

Check for a master battery switch and possibly for a second switch for the engine batteries. You should be able to use the house batteries to start the engines if the engine batteries die.

Look behind the breaker panel to see if the wiring is color-coded. Ask whether the boat is wired to American Boat and Yacht Council (ABYC) standards. This will make wiring changes less expensive because the electrician can easily determine which wires connect to which fixture.

24. The bilge pump should operate with the battery switch off. This is important. You want the bilge pump to keep pumping the boat when you are not there and the battery is turned off. Make sure that the bilge pump has a float switch, too.

25. There should be no wiring running through the bilge, but if there is, there should definitely be no wiring connections there. They can become corroded through interaction with bilge water.

26. Check that all other instruments work.

What to Look for Below Deck

27. Vents must provide adequate airflow. You want to have air circulating throughout the boat when nobody is onboard. This keeps the boat smelling fresh.

28. Look to see that the bunk sizes, number, and comfort level are acceptable.

29. Make sure that the hatches and drawers latch.

30. Check to see that the thru-valves open and close easily.

31. Check that all hoses have two hose clamps if they are below the water-line, and that hose clamps are stainless steel, not plated steel.

32. Make sure that USCG-approved fuel, heater, and stove hoses are used.

33. Look to see that water tanks have accessible valves and are vented either on deck or into the sink.

34. Make sure that fuel tanks are vented over the side, and that all valves and pipes on a fuel tank exit from the top of the tank. That way, if a line breaks, fuel does not empty into the bilge.

35. Check that the engine bilge pump and the manual bilge pump are operational.

36. Make sure that the sole boards can be lifted out easily. If you hole the hull, you may have to get them up in a hurry.

37. The bilges should be clean and dry. This is a cosmetic consideration and only tells you that the boat doesn't leak very fast. A smart owner will have pumped the bilge before you come aboard.

38. Check for signs of leaks or condensation marks on the interior paneling. Look around the front and back ends of interior windows. Check, too, under vents and air intakes.

Marine Toilet (Head)

The toilet rim should be above the water line to prevent reverse flow into the boat.

Make sure there is a proper Y-valve for overboard discharge and holding tank. Many areas require holding tanks, and installing one can be a major expense.

Engine(s)

Determine what type of shaft log the boat has and whether it should drip, or whether it is a "dripless" type.

Look at the engine water-intake lines to make sure that there are no signs of leaks from the engine raw water. Check for oil streaks, which indicate engine leaks from coolant, fuel, lubricant, or oil. In general, oil streaks from around the head gasket or crankcase gasket indicate problems.

Look for signs of oil in the coolant. Check this by shining your flashlight into the coolant before you fire up the engine. Likewise, check to see that there is no coolant in the oil by taking a look at the dipstick.

Determine that there are correct levels and clean oil in the engine and transmission. Use the dipstick.

Make sure the alternator belt fits snugly. Look for powdery deposits under the belt that show wear and misalignment.

Make sure that the engine compartment ventilation is adequate and the blowers operate.

On a gas engine installation, make sure that the vent fans work BEFORE you start the engines. Failure to do so can cause an explosion that will make your eyes water.

Any engine-driven system—bilge pump, alternator, etc.—should be working properly.

ou feel satisfied that the in-the-water items present no major problems, n it is time to look at the boat out of the water.

OUT-OF-THE-WATER CHECKLIST

The following checklist can be used on boats of all sizes, but it is primarily designed for fiberglass boats. Talk to a surveyor or boatyard to get a second opinion and to get an idea of the cost of making repairs before buying the boat.

1. Proud hull spots are caused by bulkheads installed without a foam base. Sight down the side of the boat and look for bumps running from rail to waterline. There is nothing you can do about these unless you want to repair the outside of the hull, and that is really expensive. Every boat built by the same builder may have the same problem.

2. Mismatched color indicates that damage has been repaired. If you find repaired damage, you will have to judge the quality of the repair.

3. Osmotic blisters can be a major problem. Osmotic blisters generally happen to boats that are left in the water for more than a year. Seawater penetrates the gel coat and reacts with styrene in the hull laminate, causing a blister to pop up. If you find osmotic blistering, move on to the next boat—quick. You do not want to purchase a boat on which the blisters are just developing. If the blistering has been fixed, the hull should be sound.

4. Crazing around bulkhead frame areas may indicate flexing of the hull. Again, there is nothing you can do about it.

5. Try bending or turning the rudder from under the boat to determine whether it is snug and fits well.

6. Does the rudder turn the same distance in both directions? Do both rudders turn the same amount?

7. Check the cutlass bearing to see if the shaft is in the center of the bracket or strut and if wear is present. Any wear in this area shows that the engine is out of alignment.

8. Check that the zincs are not corroded. Corroded zincs are usually the first sign of electrolysis. If so, the boat's electrical system should be checked.

9. Make sure that the brackets or struts are firmly fixed and show no signs of movement.

If you feel confident with your discoveries, discuss them with a boatyard to determine the cost of repairs. Then venture forward with a full survey.

Do You Need a Surveyor?

Buying a boat is exciting—maybe too exciting. It is easy to be so eager about the purchase of a boat that you forget to get it surveyed. Depending upon the size and age of the boat you want to buy, think about employing a marine surveyor—a professional boat evaluator. Getting your boat surveyed is like having a mechanic check on a used car that has caught your eye. Surveyors provide a professional opinion, unbiased by excitement. Simply put, the surveyor is there to help make sure that the boat is all it is advertised to be.

The notes you should have made while you were considering different boats will help to remind you of things you specifically want the surveyor to see. This will help save the surveyor's time. Go along when the boat is evaluated—and be prepared to ask questions.

Although you will receive a written report from the surveyor, be sure to take notes. The surveyor will probably take pictures during the course of the survey, but there is no reason that you can't take pictures, too, if it will help you to make up your mind.

Selecting the right surveyor

A good marine surveyor has a combination of skills that qualify him or her to evaluate boats for buyers, sellers, owners, insurance companies, and financial institutions. An experienced surveyor provides unbiased information about the value and structural condition of a boat.

Be forewarned that in most states marine surveyors are not licensed by any governmental body. There is no standard school curriculum for becoming a marine surveyor, although there are a number of correspondence and short-term programs available. The expertise of a surveyor comes from one thing: experience. An individual who has spent years sailing boats, working on boats, building boats, repairing boats, and using boats is someone who is likely to have accumulated the necessary experience and knowledge to be a marine surveyor.

Surveyors tend to specialize, so you should look for someone whose specialty is yachts or pleasure boats. Within that group, you will want someone who specializes in the type of boat construction you're considering. Wood, metal, and ferro-cement construction are particularly complex and many surveyors are not familiar with the problems they present.

Before you start, ask the surveyor what the charge will be. If you need the job done to meet insurance and financing requirements, ask if he or she is on the recommended lists of the companies you want to use. You will need to know if the insurance company wants an "in-the-water" or an "out-of-the-water" survey. Later, you should get a complete written report. You have hired this person to represent your interests, so you want an individual who will do a thorough job. Since you are paying for the survey, the document created will be your private property. The surveyor may not give the information about your report to anyone else without your permission.

The survey will evaluate the equipment, age, and condition of the boat. There will be an analysis of the problems the surveyor discovers, with a list of ways to fix them. Some of the items may be simple, such as having fire extinguishers recharged, or they can be complex, such as osmotic blistering. The surveyor will indicate market value, which may or may not reflect the need to complete the recommendations. For

⚓ **TIP**
Don't let a bad trailer discourage you from buying a good boat.

insurance purposes, the surveyor will also state the replacement value. A classic wooden yacht may have a low market value and a high replacement value, as the availability of skilled labor and materials is limited. Since the surveyor will not dismantle or open locked areas of a boat, there may be a disclaimer covering undetectable problems in inaccessible areas.

Most surveyors do not do an engine survey. They can make recommendations about taking engine oil samples for analysis and give you the names of people who will survey an engine. If you are buying a high-powered boat with expensive engines, get them looked at by a professional engine mechanic/surveyor.

There are three national organizations of **marine surveyors**:

The National Association of Marine Surveyors (NAMS) is the oldest. Applicants to NAMS must have been solely employed as surveyors for a period of years and must pass a written examination before they are admitted. Attendance at an annual conference is required to maintain membership status.

The Society of Accredited Marine Surveyors (SAMS) will accept new surveyors and provide some training courses.

Both organizations maintain geographic membership lists and toll-free numbers so you can easily locate a surveyor in your area. Or visit their Web sites: www.nams-cms.org or www.marinesurvey.org.

The Association of Marine Surveyors (ACMS) requires that surveyors have at least five years of work experience before registering with ACMS. The group has a certification program and holds annual programs and meetings. It's on the Web at www.acms-usa.com.

Surveys are valuable

When you buy a new boat, the bill of sale and commissioning information may satisfy the insurance and lending institutions. However, you will usually need a survey. New boats that are shipped a great distance, across country or across an ocean, may sustain damage in transit. In this case, the shipper or boat builder may pay for the survey.

Regulations and building practices vary from country to country. For a foreign-built boat, check with the dealer or get a surveyor to verify that it complies with U.S. regulations. When you take possession of your new boat, you may want a factory expert and an independent surveyor with you for a test sail. A surveyor's report will help you should warranty problems become an issue later.

When purchasing a used boat, you should have access to existing surveys. Ask the owner or broker if you can look at them. An old survey is not a substitute for your own report, but it is an indicator of the boat's history. It may list equipment that is not onboard or recommendations that were never acted upon. It is one more tool to help you make a wise decision about your purchase.

CHAPTER 5

TRY BEFORE YOU BUY

Whether you are buying a new or used boat, you should ask for a test ride or a sea trial before completing the deal. This is not an unusual request and most reasonable sellers will agree to it. If you are buying a used boat, it's a good idea to bring an experienced friend along, too. A sea trial can be as simple as a quick spin around the harbor or as involved as an all-day event.

The Sea Trial

You wake up on the morning of your sea trial to a cloudless day with blue sky and no wind. A perfect day for the trial? Yes. A flat calm will enable you to get a good feel for the boat's performance in terms of cruise and top speed. Plus, if the wind is normally flat calm in your area until later in the day, you'll be operating in normal conditions. But you'll learn even more about the ride and handling of the boat if you go out later in the day or a second time when there is a little wind and sea.

Put the boat through its paces

When you get to the dock, look to see how the boat floats. Is the waterline submerged? Is the boat trimmed down by the stern? Does it have a list? A submerged waterline means that either the line was painted in the wrong place or that the owner added a lot of gear. If it's the latter, expect the performance to be degraded appropriately. If the boat has a list, there's nothing you can do about it unless you rearrange gear to eliminate the list. If the boat is down by the stern, ask if this is normal. If not, you may want to look for stores placed well aft, a leak, or another reason.

Step aboard and take a walk around the boat. Get a feel for whether the handholds are in the right place, and whether there is good visibility from the helm station. Stand at the wheel and look down at the dock. Can you see the dock edge? Can you see the mooring lines?

Make sure that you're on board when the engine is started for the first time that day. You'll never find out that the engine has trouble starting if the owner has warmed it up before you get there. Check the temperature gauges to make sure they're cold before anyone flips the starting switch.

Before the boat leaves the dock, look at the exhaust. A cold engine will make a little smoke, but the newer fuel-injected engines produce very little smoke after a minute or two. Check the cooling water coming from the engine or engines. On twin engine boats, both engines should spew the same color and amount of exhaust and the same levels of cooling water. Wait for the engines to warm up and the thermostats to open, and then check the temperature gauges. They should not exceed 180 degrees.

Listen to the noise levels. If you cannot make yourself heard over the sound of the engine, you may end up suffering ear damage after a day on the water. You should be able to talk in a normal voice.

Leaving the dock

The seller will probably want to steer the boat away from the dock. But once it's in open water, you should be able to take over. The first thing you'll want to ask the owner about is cruising speed. This is the speed at which the boat will go for long periods without overheating or undue stress and is about 70% to 80% of the boat's top speed. Check to see that the cruising speed is consistent with the advertised speed.

Once the boat is clear of the dock, ask to take the helm. Get clear of the dock and put it astern. Observe whether the stern swings in one direction or the other. Single props generally swing to port when going astern. Keep running the boat astern for a moment and see how well the boat tracks in a straight line. Back off on the throttles and put the boat in neutral. Let it coast for a moment to see if it goes in a straight line. Put the engine in ahead and gently increase the rpms about a hundred rpms at a time. Let the boat settle between each step. As soon as the boat has settled down at the new rpms, make a note of the speed, rpms, and noise levels. Run the boat out of the harbor. Once clear of the no-wake zone, run the boat at just under planing speed and get a feel for the trim angle. While you are in this condition, check visibility from the helm position.

> ### ⚓ T I P
> Twin engines represent double security—just one of them can get you home. But at $10,000 to $14,000 per engine, they're also twice as expensive!

Occasionally, boats trim up so far by the bow that you cannot see ahead when the boat is in the semi-displacement mode. Now crank it up to speed and use a portable Global Positioning System (GPS) to read off the boat's speed. Allow a few minutes for the GPS to give you a handle on the speed and check it against the speed on the boat's gauges. If you don't have a GPS, you can always run a measured mile, as long as you know where the measured mile markers are and can keep the boat going at a consistent speed through the distance.

Back off to cruise speed and run the boat across the seas to get a feel for its stability. Make a turn and run downwind. The most difficult condition for a powerboat to run in is downwind at about the same speed as the waves. Quite often, boats will surf down the back of a wave and the steering will become mushy. This is the precursor to a broach. While this doesn't happen very often, finding out what the boat does before you buy it is a worthwhile exercise.

Once you have performed all the evolutions, slow down, turn off one engine and see if the boat can be steered on one engine. Some boats can't, but if an engine fails, you may have to motor home on one engine. So try it now before you buy the boat.

So far, so good...

If you are happy with the trial so far and you are planning to use the boat for offshore fishing, it's time to try going astern in a seaway. (This maneuver should ONLY be attempted by an experienced boater. If you try it, be extremely careful, because if you do it wrong you can flood the cockpit and sink the boat.) Put the boat astern into the waves and GENTLY increase the throttles. If the stern shows any tendency to submerge, stop immediately. Don't go astern too long or too fast. Bring the engine rpms down and go ahead.

You can also try a few hard turns to see how the boat handles them. Most boats heel inward on a turn, but one or two heel outward. This can be disconcerting if you do not expect it. Now give the helm back to the owner and let him or her drive it back into harbor while you check the onboard deck systems.

Look first at the bridge systems. If you are on the flying bridge, make sure the radar operates sufficiently far enough above you that you are not getting zapped with radar waves every time the antenna turns. Turn the radar on and make sure that you can see to the horizon on the screen in all states of trim. Occasionally, you'll find that the radar range becomes limited astern as the boat trims up by the stern. You get a good view of the boat's wake, but you'll miss the freighter coming up astern. Check the depth sounder against the chart to get a feel for its accuracy. If the boat has a fish finder, slow down and try it in an area where you know there are fish. Check visibility on all the other instruments. Especially note which screens are hard to read. Many Liquid Crystal Display (LCD) screens are difficult to read in direct sunlight.

Now go below and check out the interior. Look to see if handholds are within reach and if you can move easily through the boat. Sit on the forward bunk or seat and get a feel for how hard the ride is. If you bounce off the seat in a small sea it is too hard! Check noise levels below. If you can't hear yourself think, you may have to invest in sound insulation.

Back on deck

Now go back on deck. If you are buying a fishing boat, walk around the boat with a fishing pole to make sure that nothing obstructs your pole. Check to see where the props are in relation to your fishing rod. Outboard props and stern drives are notorious for snagging fishing lines. If you troll, set up a rod and make sure everything works as expected. If the sea trial is satisfactory, it's time to get the survey and purchase details worked out.

> **TIP**
>
> Can you handle routine engine and electrical repairs? If not, get a new boat—not a used one.

Chartering as a trial

If you're interested in a new boat, the actual boat you're going to buy might not be available for a trial. In that case, the dealer or seller may offer an identical vessel for the day. Your preliminary offer on the boat should include the stipulation that the performance of the two boats will be consistent. However, boat builders offer many different engine options. The boat you try may have a different engine from the one you buy and this will affect performance and handling.

If you cannot get a boat for a sea trial, yet another option is to charter an identical boat for the day. However, charter operators will not let a novice climb into a boat and take off. You might hire someone to operate the boat, or you could bring an experienced friend or family member along. Either way, once the boat is underway, you should be able to take the wheel for a while in open water. You can learn a lot about how a boat handles in just a short period of time.

If you want to get a feel for a boat's capabilities as a cruiser, you could also arrange for an on-dock or on-the-water weekend charter. Spending a weekend tied up at a dock might not sound exciting, but it will give you an idea of what it might be like to be aboard with another adult and a couple of kids for any length of time on your boat. If you can meander around your favorite cruising grounds for a weekend, you will know exactly how your new boat will fit into the family cruising experience.

PART II

OUTFITTING

After you have purchased your boat, you will probably need to fit it out. First, you should make sure you have all the safety features required by law, then you should add some useful gear such as fenders, anchors, and lines. Only after you have the essentials onboard should you think about what gear will enhance your boating experience.

CHAPTER 6

STAYING SAFE

A ccording to the U.S. Coast Guard (USCG), several hundred lives could be saved each year if every boater were to wear a life jacket. Although your safety depends on the type of boat you use and the nature of the boating that you do, the regulations on USCG-approved safety equipment are mandatory for all boats. It is your legal responsibility to carry the required equipment listed on pages 86 to 91, to keep that equipment in proper working order, and to operate your boat in a safe manner.

PERSONAL FLOTATION DEVICES

On any boating trip there is a chance that someone will fall overboard or that the boat will sink. In case of either event, a personal flotation device (PFD), otherwise known as a life jacket, is designed to keep your head above water and assist you in maintaining a position that permits proper breathing.

Everyone aboard the boat needs a PFD. Children should wear PFDs at all times. In some states, the law states that all children six and under must wear them while onboard; in other states, it is all children under twelve. Adult non-swimmers, anyone boating alone, anyone wearing a cast, or anyone who must do a job that could result in being swept overboard must wear a PFD whenever the boat is underway.

The USCG classifies PFDs into five types. (In Europe, Safety of Life at Sea- (SOLAS-) approved lifejackets that offer up to 35 pounds of buoyancy are the norm.) The USCG-approved categories are:

► Type I

A Type I PFD is the easiest to pull on in an emergency. It provides the most buoyancy and is effective for all waters, especially open, rough, or remote waters requiring extended survival. It is designed to turn most unconscious wearers to a face-up position. Type I is available in jacket or bib models, as shown. The adult size provides at least 22 pounds of buoyancy; the child size, 11 pounds minimum.

► Type II

The Type II "horse-collar" or near-shore buoyant vest is intended for calm, inland water or wherever there is a good chance of quick rescue. The turning action is not as pronounced or as effective for as many people as Type I. An adult size provides at least $15\frac{1}{2}$ pounds of buoyancy; a medium child size provides 11 pounds. Infant and small child sizes each provide at least 7 pounds of buoyancy.

► Type III

The Type III is generally the most comfortable and popular type of PFD. It's made of foam, rather than the more bulky kapok, and is available in many styles, colors, and sizes. Also known as a flotation aid, a Type III PFD is good for calm, inland water, or where there is a good chance of a quick rescue. It has the same minimum buoyancy as Type II. However, the wearer may have to tilt the head back to avoid turning face down in the water.

► Type IV

The Type IV is a throwable device designed for calm inland water with heavy boat traffic where help is always present. It is not designed to be worn, but rather to be thrown to a person in the water, then grasped and held by the user until the rescue occurs. Type IV devices include horseshoe buoys (approved for use in the U.S.), ring buoys, and buoyant cushions.

► Type V

The Type V is the least bulky of all PFD types. It contains a small amount of inherent buoyancy and an inflatable chamber. When it is inflated, its performance is equal to a Type I, II, or III PFD. USCG regulations also recognize certain Type V special-purpose devices, including wet suits, deck suits, and whitewater types.

► Inflatable lifejackets

Inflatable lifejackets are officially classified as Type VI and have become extremely popular. They fit like a normal collar with the vest folded inside the collar. If the wearer goes over the side, the jacket can either be manually inflated or can inflate automatically. Manually inflated jackets operate with a simple tug on a lanyard. This sets off the compressed air cylinder and the lifejacket fills. You need to be conscious to operate the lanyard. Auto-inflating jackets operate as soon as the igniter tablet gets wet.

In addition to PFDs and fire extinguishers, flame arresters, sound signaling devices, and visual distress signals are also legally required by the USCG. *Indicates items required by the USCG.

Bilge pump or bailer

Although federal regulations do not require dewatering devices—a bucket or other bailer on unpowered boats or electric bilge pumps on boats with engines— they are required by some state laws. Required or not, these items are recommended for safe boating. The Ocean Racing Council (ORC) recommends that boats have at least two bilge pumps, one of which is operable from the cockpit. Most manufacturers use the ORC recommendations as a basic standard.

Boathook

A hook on a pole is invaluable for fending off, placing lines over pilings, picking up pennants of mooring buoys, and recovering articles dropped over the side. When marked with rings at one-foot intervals—a mark in a different color or size should be added for the boat's draft—a boathook is useful for probing around a stranded boat in search of deeper water.

Charts and navigation publications

Essential for planning your course and navigating safely, charts and navigation publications, such as those covered in Chapter 9, should be up to date. For planning your trip, you can use an electronic chart on your home computer. These charts are as extensive as, and in some cases, more extensive than paper charts. Their cost is around $100 to $250 depending on manufacturer.

Compass

Desirable on any boat for both emergency and regular use, a compass and plotting instruments are recommended for piloting purposes.

Detectors and alarms

A well-thought-out alarm system can alert you to a wide variety of dangers, from burglars on deck to explosive vapors trapped below.

A float switch mounted above the normal bilge-water level can signal flooding in the bilge and turn on the bilge pump. Other detectors indicate dangerous levels of gasoline, propane, hydrogen fumes, or carbon monoxide. Additional sensors can warn of low oil pressure, loss of engine coolant, and fire. For detecting burglars coming aboard, neither home nor automobile alarms are practical aboard an occupied boat; only install an alarm that is specifically designed for marine use.

Very High Frequency (VHF) radio

The VHF radio is the most basic piece of electronic safety equipment used on boats. It can receive weather reports, Coast Guard warnings, and messages. It can be used to call for assistance. See Chapter 9 for a description of other electronic equipment that you may want to have on board.

Emergency Position Indicating Radio Beacon (EPIRB)

This automatic radio transmitter, described in Chapter 9, should be carried on any boat operating offshore.

Fenders

Carried in appropriate sizes and numbers, fenders are used for normal berthing, and when two boats must make fast to each other while underway or at anchor.

First-aid kit

An essential item of safety equipment, the kit, described in Chapter 10, should be accompanied by a first-aid manual and supplemented by one or more first-aid courses.

Flame arrester*

With some minor and technical exceptions, every inboard gasoline engine must be equipped with an acceptable means of backfire flame control—or "flame arrester." Flame arresters no longer require USCG approval; the USCG now accepts flame arresters complying with Underwriters Laboratories (UL) Standard 1111 or Society of Automotive Engineers (SAE) J1928. When in use, flame arresters must be secured to the air intake of the carburetor with an airtight connection. Elements must be clean, and grids must be tight enough to prevent flames from passing through. Note that many engines are now using Electronic Fuel Injection (EFI), which eliminates the need for a flame arrester.

TIP

Always listen to a weather broadcast before going on board. On the water, your VHF can pick up the National Oceanic & Atmospheric Administration (NOAA) broadcasts on WX-1, WX-2, or WX-3 stations.

Flashlight or searchlight

A searchlight—installed on larger craft, hand-held on smaller boats—serves both as a night piloting aid and as an emergency signaling device. A multi-cell flashlight or electric lantern can serve these functions, although sometimes less effectively.

Ground tackle

Ground tackle includes anchors, anchor rode (line or chain) and all the shackles and other anchoring gear. All ground tackle must be in operational condition. After use, it should be carefully re-stowed so that the main anchor is ready for use and auxiliary and storm anchors are readily accessible.

Leadline

A hand-held leadline is useful as a backup to the electronic depth sounder. For help in choosing the right anchor, affix a dollop of wax or hard grease to the bottom of the lead to obtain a sample of bottom material.

Life rafts

Standards for life rafts—size, capacity ratings, seaworthiness, sturdiness—are set by SOLAS international conventions, and are adapted for the U.S. by the USCG. For everyone who sails offshore, a SOLAS-approved inflatable life raft should be considered mandatory. For racing boats, ORC regulations insist on SOLAS-approved lifejackets.

Lightning protection

Lightning strikes a number of boats every year, especially in Florida and other southern states. Lightning protection aboard your boat could help avoid considerable damage to your boat and may save the lives of those aboard. Two types of lightning protection should be installed—one to guide the charge of a main strike safely down into the water, the other to protect electronic equipment from a damaging power surge.

In recent years the thinking about boats and lightning strikes has changed. It is now believed that a bottle-brush style ion dissipator helps to disperse the ions that cause lightning in the first place. Dissipator manufacturers claim that boats using a dissipator have never been struck by lightning.

SAFETY EQUIPMENT

Sound signaling devices*

The *Navigation Rules* require sound signals to be made under certain cir-cumstances, including meeting, crossing, and overtaking other boats. (These situations are described in detail in the *Rules*.) All vessels, including recreational vessels, are required to sound fog signals during periods of reduced visibility. So, you must have on board some means of making an efficient sound signal. Vessels 39.4 feet or more in length are required to carry on board a whistle (horn) for marine use and a bell. In an emergency, you can use any loud noise to attract attention. Use a loud hailer, or make a megaphone from a rolled up chart, or bang on a metal pot.

Spare parts and tools

The list of tools and spare parts to be carried on board is best developed by skippers for their own boats. It will vary, depending on the type of boat, how it is normally used, and the capabilities of the crew. The list may include items for making emergency repairs at sea, such as simple tools, plugs, cloth, screws, nails, wire, and tape. Spare bulbs for the navigation lights, and various mechanical and electrical spare parts may also be included.

Visual distress signals*

Most boats—and all boats operating offshore and on the Great Lakes—must be equipped with visual distress signals. These are classified by the USCG for day use only (D), night use only (N), or combined day-and-night use (D/N). If pyrotechnic signals are used, the minimum quantity is three each of D and N signals, or three D/N signals. Each device must be readily accessible and certified as complying with USCG requirements. Replace distress and smoke flares, and meteor rockets after 42 months from the date of manufacture.

USCG regulations prohibit any display of visual distress signals, except when assistance is required. Use emergency signals only when in distress, and only when help is close enough to see the signal.

ACR Electronics has a special light called the SOSearchlight. It flashes an SOS signal that is visible for over 18 miles at night. The SOS light can run for hours on one battery. It is approved by the USCG.

On board a boat, fire extinguishers are required if one or more of the following conditions exist:

► There are inboard or inboard/outboard engines on the boat.

► There are closed compartments where fuel tanks are stored.

► There are closed stowage compartments in which flammable or combustable materials are stored.

► There are double bottoms that are not sealed to the hull or are not completely filled with flotation materials.

► There are closed living spaces.

► The boat has permanently installed fuel tanks.

Approved extinguishers are classified by a letter and number symbol. Type B, commonly used on boats, is designed to put out fires involving flammable liquids such as gasoline, oil, and grease. BI and BII extinguishers both contain foam, CO_2, dry chemicals, or non-flammable gas. Just like PFDs, extinguishers should be easily accessible.

FIRE EXTINGUISHER CONTENTS				
Class	Foam in gals.	CO_2 in lbs.	Dry Chemical in lbs.	Halon in lbs.
B-I	1.25	4	2	2.5
B-II	2.50	15	10	10.0

Fueling

Fueling the boat properly is an essential element of good seamanship. Whether you are planning a day's outing or an extended cruise, before starting out make sure you have enough fuel on board and, if any is needed, that you fill the tank safely. Practice the "one-third rule": Use one-third of your fuel going out, one-third to get back, and keep one-third in reserve.

Of primary importance is the condition of your fuel tanks. If you have portable fuel tanks, make sure that they are constructed of sturdy material and in good condition, that they are free of excessive corrosion, and that they do not leak. The vents on portable tanks must be operable; the tanks themselves should have a vapor-tight, leakproof cap.

When you fuel a gasoline-powered boat, make sure all motors and galley flames are turned off and that a fire extinguisher is close at hand.

TIP

When fueling your boat, wipe the area around the fuel fill with a soapy sponge before you undo the fill. That way if any fuel spills, the soapy area will prevent it from soaking into or staining the deck.

Boat registration

All powerboats must be registered in the state of primary use. You can get the numbers and license at the state tax collector's office. A boat number begins with a two-letter state designation, followed by not more than four digits and not more than two letters. Between the letter and number groups there must be a hyphen or space. Numbers should be displayed in bold block letters on both sides of the boat's forward half. States usually require that a validation sticker, confirming that registration fees have been paid, be displayed with the numbers.

TIP

Don't drink and drive! Boating while intoxicated (BWI) is against the law, just like DWI. So save that bottle of Dom Perignon for dry land. On the water, keep your head clear.

Safety On Board

From the moment you begin to plan your boating excursion to the moment you return, there are steps you can take to ensure that everyone on board has a safe trip. Planning starts with a float plan written before you even leave. It tells someone on shore where you are going and when you plan to return. You should instruct that person to call the Coast Guard within half an hour to an hour after your scheduled return if you have not reported that you are home. If you are going to be in a different port each night, check in with your shore base each night to let them know of your arrival time and any change in plans. If the weather deteriorates, be sure to call or check in as soon as possible.

PRE-DEPARTURE FLOAT PLAN

1. **NAME AND PHONE NUMBER OF PERSON REPORTING**

2. **DESCRIPTION OF BOAT** Type of boat; hull, deck, and cabin color; trim; registration number; length; name of boat; make; any other distinguishing features.

3. **PERSONS ABOARD** Name, age, address, telephone number of skipper and each crew member.

4. **MEDICAL PROBLEMS OF ANY PERSON ABOARD**

5. **ENGINE TYPE** Horsepower, number of engines, fuel capacity.

6. **SAFETY AND SURVIVAL EQUIPMENT** Personal flotation devices, flares, mirror, visual distress signals, flashlight, food, paddles, water supply, anchor, life raft, dinghy, and EPIRB and any other safety equipment aboard.

7. **MARINE RADIO** Type, frequencies.

8. **TRIP EXPECTATIONS** Departure points, route, destination, expected date and time of arrival. Expected date of return.

9. **VEHICLE LICENSES** Color, make, and license number of automobile and trailer (if applicable), and where they are parked.

10. **SUGGESTED DATE AND TIME TO CALL COAST GUARD OR LOCAL AUTHORITY FOR SEARCH**

11. **TELEPHONE NUMBERS TO CALL FOR FURTHER INFORMATION OR IN CASE OF EMERGENCY**

12. **COMPETENCY OF PEOPLE ABOARD** Boating skills and emergency first-aid training.

Loading and capacity

The weight of people, fuel, and gear that can safely be carried on a boat is referred to as its loading and capacity. The USCG issues capacity plates to manufacturers of monohull boats less than 20 feet long, except for sailboats, canoes, kayaks, and inflatables. It includes information on the maximum number of persons and maximum weight of persons or persons and gear that can safely be carried on the boat. In boats powered by outboards, it includes the maximum horsepower capacity. For boats over 20 feet long, there are some voluntary industry standards, but the USCG regulations do not apply.

TIP

Be wary of overloading your boat. It is a major cause of boating accidents.

▲ **Never overload your boat—it's a major cause of boating accidents. And it can turn a minor mishap while boating into a major disaster. Check a boat's capacity before loading.**

BOATING SAFETY CHECKLIST

Is your boat as safe as it can possibly be? If you can answer "Yes" to the following questions, chances are that the vessel is safely equipped and that you operate it safely.

- ► Do you carry legally required and other safety equipment aboard, and do you know how to use it?

- ► Before getting underway, do you review emergency procedures and identify all safety equipment and exits with everyone aboard?

- ► If you carry a life raft on board your boat, have you included the proper deployment as part of your routine safety training? At least one other crew member should know, for example, where the raft is located, how to inflate it quickly, and to inflate it on deck rather than below deck or in the cockpit.

- ► Are you aware that it is illegal to operate a vessel while intoxicated? Most states use .08 ppm as the maximum blood-alcohol level for recreational boaters. However, the USCG still has to make the arrest. When alcohol or drugs are mixed with boating, the results can be fatal. A large percentage of all boating accidents are alcohol-related.

- ► Do you check local weather reports before departure and keep the VHF NOAA weather radio on, as well as keep a weather eye open during your sail? Do you know what different types of clouds mean?

- ► Are your lifesaving equipment and fire extinguishers readily accessible at all times?

- ► Do you avoid overloading your boat with people or gear?

- ► Do you make sure you have good, non-skid surfaces on deck and on the soles of the shoes of everyone on board?

- ► Do you keep bilges clean and electrical contacts tight?

- ► Do you guard rigidly against any fuel system leakage?

- ► Have you requested a USCG Auxiliary Courtesy Marine Examination for the current year?

▶ Have you taken any safe-boating courses or first-aid courses?

▶ Before departing, do you leave a float plan so that someone knows where you are going and when you are expected to return? Do you notify the holder if plans change?

▶ Are you familiar with the waters that you will be cruising, so that you can deal with tides, currents, sandbars, and any other hazards you may encounter?

▶ Do you know your personal limitations and responsibilities? Remember that exposure to sun, wind, and cold water affect your ability to react.

▶ Do you check power line clearances while underway?

▶ If you are a non-swimmer, are you planning to learn to swim? It could save your life or someone else's.

▶ Are you and your crew prepared for any emergencies that could occur?

▶ Do you watch, and heed, posted speed limits? Do you slow down in anchorages?

▶ When anchoring, do you allow adequate scope? Are you far enough away from neighboring boats?

▶ If someone falls into the water, do you know what to do? Avoid jumping in; use a reaching, throwing, or floating assist such as a paddle, a cushion, a Type IV PFD life ring, or a rescue line with a float attached.

▶ Do you avoid relieving yourself over the side of the boat in a standing position? This is a common cause of falling off the boat.

▶ Do you know that standing in a small boat raises the center of gravity, often to the point of capsizing? Standing for any reason or even changing position in a small boat can be dangerous, as is sitting on the gunwales or seat backs or in a pedestal seat while underway.

TEN STEPS TO SAFETY MAINTENANCE

Most marine safety equipment needs some sort of maintenance. This can range from regular, ongoing attention, to periodic checks at weekly, monthly, or annual intervals. Following the guidelines below, custom design a checklist for your particular boat, adding to it as you install or modify equipment. Make an entry in the boat's log of all inspections, tests, and servicing of fire extinguishers. Not only will this record essential checks; it may prove valuable for insurance surveys or claims. Remember, just as important as making periodic checks is actually performing follow-up repair. Never delay maintenance related to safety, and avoid operating a boat that has any safety defect.

1. Keep your bilge absolutely free of dirt and trash. Check frequently and clean it out as often as needed. Accumulations of dirt, sawdust, wood chips, and trash in the bilge will soak up oil and fuel drippings. In addition to creating a fire hazard, this may also clog limber holes—drainage holes— and bilge pumps.

2. Inspect lifesaving equipment. At the beginning and mid-point of each boating season, check the condition of lifesaving equipment (see pages 86 to 91). Replace substandard lifesaving devices immediately. Attempt repairs only where full effectiveness can be restored; if in doubt, ask for USCG advice.

3. Discharge a fire extinguisher periodically, as a test. In addition to good maintenance, this provides valuable practice. Discharge one of the portable units each year on a regular rotation basis—preferably in the form of a drill with all crew members participating. On shore, put out an actual small fire in a metal pan or tub. When discharging a CO_2 extinguisher, always hold the nozzle by the plastic handle; never unscrew the hose from the cylinder to discharge it openly. Always discharge a dry-chemical extinguisher completely.

After an extinguisher has been removed for testing or practice discharge, have it serviced by a competent shop and reinstalled as soon as possible.

Make sure that there are always enough extinguishers aboard to serve your boat's safety needs.

4. Check the engine and fuel system frequently for cleanliness and leaks. If you find any leaks, take immediate action. Wipe up any oil or grease drippings and stop leaks as soon as possible. Do not use the boat, and—with all loads turned off so that no sparks will jump—disconnect the leads from the battery so that the engine cannot be started.

5. Check the entire fuel system annually, inch by inch, including fuel lines in areas not normally visible. When replacing fuel system components, use equivalent replacement parts—never automotive parts. If any joints or lengths of tubing or hose are worn or damaged, call a qualified mechanic without delay.

6. Have a qualified professional inspect your boat's electrical system thoroughly every year, including all wiring in areas not normally visible.

Search for any cut or chafed insulation, corrosion at connections, excessive sag or strain on conductors, and other visible signs of deterioration. Test leakage by opening each circuit at the main distribution panel, with all loads turned off, and measure current flow. Ideally, there should be no current flow; current of more than a few milliamperes indicates electrical leakage that should be identified and corrected without delay.

Keep in mind that connections at the boat's storage batteries need special attention. Disconnect them and, using a wire brush, remove all corrosion. Next, replace and tighten the connections, then apply a light coat of grease or other protective substance.

7. Maintain your boat's bilge ventilation system in top operating condition.

8. Check underwater fittings annually. This includes shafts, propellers, rudders, struts, stuffing boxes and metal skegs. Repack stuffing boxes as often as necessary to keep them from leaking excessively, while also checking shafting for alignment and excessive wear at strut bearings. Examine propellers to see if they need truing up.

TEN STEPS TO SAFETY MAINTENANCE

9. Choose replacement parts carefully. Whatever parts you replace—for fuel, electrical or ventilation systems, navigation light bulbs, or anything else aboard your boat—make sure you use equivalent components that are designed specifically for marine use.

10. Perform an annual safety inspection of the hull and fittings below the waterline. On wooden boats, check hull planking for physical damage and for any general deterioration from age. Check fiberglass hulls for any cracks, especially at points of high stress. Call in an expert if you find any suspicious areas.

You should **test all PFDs** periodically to make sure they have retained their buoyancy. The most instructive way of doing this is by putting one on and jumping into a pool or shallow water. Not only will this test each lifejacket, but it will give you some experience of getting into one and using it. This is especially important for inflatable jackets. (It is very hard to read the instructions after you have fallen off the boat.) After every use, wash the lifejacket with fresh water. Always air-dry your PFDs thoroughly. Store them in a dry, well-ventilated, easily accessible place on the boat during summer and off the boat during the long months of winter storage.

S easickness is important to know about and understand. If you get seasick, your trips may be no fun at all. If you get severely sick whenever you go on a boat, you may be best off moving inland and taking up gardening. If you've never been on a boat, it is essential to discover how your system reacts.

If you are always seasick, then consider the circumstances. Think about what kind of boat have you been on. Some boats roll more than others and even the best boaters feel queasy. Ask yourself what you ate before you went out. Greasy or alcoholic foods can contribute to seasickness. Some people have inner-ear problems and suffer from motion sickness. Find out what category you fit into. If you only get seasick in very windy and lumpy conditions, you can probably find a cure. If you get seasick walking down the dock—again, stay ashore and tend the roses.

The most important thing to recognize is that seasickness is real and that the symptoms can lead to serious problems. Seasickness should not be ignored, because vomiting will lead to dehydration. Small quantities of liquid should be drunk. Soda crackers or similar solids should be eaten as often as possible. Anyone with regular seasickness should avoid alcohol the night before and during the outing.

TIP

If you suffer from dehydration, get medical attention quickly.

Overcoming seasickness is largely a matter of your body's sensory system readjusting to being on water. Often this readjustment will take a day or two of continual time on board. Because you usually live on land, your senses have to learn new patterns when you are on the water. First, try to get aboard the boat the night before you are going on a trip. That way you can sleep aboard and start to acclimate your system to being afloat. Watch what you eat before you head out. Eggs and bacon may be a wonderful breakfast on board, but not if you get seasick. Have some dry toast, a bagel, or a muffin. Avoid stimulants such as coffee or tea. You might also wish to discuss anti-nausea medication options with a healthcare professional.

CHAPTER 7

NUTS AND BOLTS

New boats often come with no additional equipment, and you have to purchase all your gear. While most used boats come with a lot of equipment, you may still have to buy some additional gear. In this chapter, you'll learn about some of the equipment you should have on board and some that will make your boating experience more enjoyable.

GROUND TACKLE

Because heavy anchors are so difficult to handle and raise, the aim in anchor design has been to develop a relatively lightweight anchor that digs itself into the bottom. Today's anchors have features that enable them to stay put without excessive weight.

The **holding power** of an anchor is a value given to it by the manufacturer, but in practice, holding power depends on many factors and can vary tremendously. For example, a Danforth anchor may not have the weight to penetrate a pebble bottom and may have little or no holding power in this situation. On the other hand, some anchors snag cables or debris on the ocean floor and cannot be pulled out. They have tremendous holding power in that situation. Holding power should be taken as an indication of an anchor's potential, not as a hard and fast fact.

Types of anchors

There are many different types of anchors on the market, but they all have certain features in common. Each anchor has flukes, a stock, a shank or shaft, and is of a certain weight. In general, the larger the flukes, the better the anchor will hold. If you are fitting out a small boat, you should have at least one anchor on board. It will probably be a Danforth, Fortress, Bruce, or plow-style anchor to give you the largest range of use. As you buy a larger boat, you will need to have at least two anchors on board and should invest in a wider variety of anchors for more specific anchoring problems.

Danforth or fluke anchor

Developed in 1938 by R. D. Ogg and R. S. Danforth, the lightweight Danforth anchor is made of two flat steel or aluminum flukes that dig into the bottom of the sea. It is especially effective in mud, sand, or clay, although it sometimes skips over rocky bottoms. This style of anchor is available from Fortress (you can adjust the fluke angle on the Fortress for better holding in soft mud), Simpson-Lawrence, and other manufacturers now that the Danforth patent has expired. The foldable design makes it easy to stow and easy to use.

Fortress anchor

Fortress anchors are similar to Danforths with a couple of differences. Fortress anchors can be taken apart for easier stowage in their own bag. The angle of their fluke can be adjusted to enable the anchor to dig in more deeply. At the most extreme angle, the flukes of a Fortress anchor can be set at 45 degrees for better holding power.

Plow anchor

The plow anchor was originally invented by Sir Geoffrey Taylor in the 1930s. He named it the CQR or "Secure" anchor, by which name it is sometimes known. It looks just like a plow, with a large, almost triangular fluke that pivots at the end of a shank. The fluke buries itself into soft bottoms and has excellent holding power. Because they're relatively heavy and bulky (the lightest start at 15 pounds), they are best for larger boats (25 feet or more.) They are usually stored on bow rollers.

The Delta

A new plow-shaped anchor from Simpson-Lawrence, is made in one piece and can be used instead of a plow or Danforth for mud, shale, sandy, and silt bottoms.

Bruce anchor

This anchor was originally developed in Britain in the 1950s for use with offshore oil and gas drilling rigs. Scaled down for recreational use, it can right itself no matter how it lands on the bottom. It works well on mud, sand, or rocks.

Max anchor

The broad flukes of the Max anchor give it greater holding power. Since its shank is adjustable, the angle can be increased for soft bottoms.

Fisherman anchor

The Fisherman anchor looks like the traditional anchor with upturned arms and small flukes, but it often goes by different names. If it has diamond-shaped flukes it might be called a Herreschoff anchor. With spear-shaped flukes it is known as the Nicholson anchor. The Yachtsman anchor has triangular flukes. It is useful for hard, rocky bottoms or bottoms with lots of weeds or grass. It is heavier than a burying-type anchor.

Kedge anchor

A kedge anchor is a small anchor used to warp the boat from one berth to another. But the name is commonly applied to any type of small anchor used for short periods of time.

Grapnel anchor

The grapnel or grappling anchor has five curved prongs around a central shank. It is best used on wrecks and should be considered a throwaway because it is very hard to retrieve once it has hooked the wreck. It can also be dragged along the bottom to retrieve lost anchor lines.

Mushroom anchor

The mushroom anchor looks like an upside-down mushroom. Since it takes these anchors a long time to dig into the bottom, they can only be used with vessels 15 feet long or smaller. For short periods of time, they're especially good for inflatables, canoes, and rowboats. Mushroom anchors that have been buried in the bottom are also used as part of a permanent mooring system, along with a chain and buoy.

The number of anchors you should carry depends upon several things: the type of anchors used, the size of your boat, and whether you are boating only in familiar, sheltered waters or cruising to many harbors.

Many boats carry two anchors, with the weight of the heavier one about one-and-a-half times the weight of the lighter one. For cruising boats, a third anchor is helpful to have because it will allow you to use whatever anchor suits the bottom. Typically, a boat may carry a single anchor (a Bruce, Danforth, Fortress, or plow style gives the most flexibility) on the bow roller. This anchor will be suitable for

⚓ **T I P**

Remember: you must drop anchor whenever you stop for lunch, fishing, or scuba diving.

anchoring for brief stops—for example, an afternoon or for lunch. The heavier anchor (also a Bruce or plow style) should be used if you intend anchoring overnight. Most powerboats do not have a second bow roller, so the heavier anchor will usually be stowed below deck. If you decide to carry a third anchor, it should be a fisherman-style anchor, in case you decide to anchor in rock-strewn areas. No anchor will hold reliably on rock bottoms, although you might snag a rock for a while.

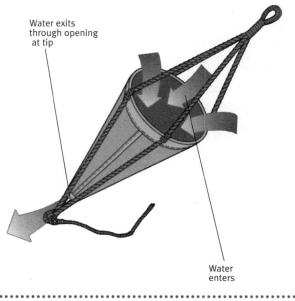

Water exits through opening at tip

Water enters

▲ A floating sea anchor, or drogue, trails behind the boat and slows it down. It is useful for anglers and sailors who want to keep their stem going straight ahead in rough seas.

Now that you have your anchor, you're almost ready to anchor your boat. **How much anchor line do you need?** You'll need to have some idea of the areas in which you'll anchor and how much scope is required— that is, the length of anchor line you need to let out when compared to the depth of water.

Anchors are most secure when the angle of the anchor line is as close to the horizontal as possible. However, that might mean that you will have to pay out a huge amount of line. If you have a chain near the anchor, it serves to keep the anchor line nearly horizontal. Generally, depending on the conditions, you can use more or less scope, but the absolute minimum is about five to one. (That is, the anchor line is five times the water depth.) You might only use this scope if you were anchoring for lunch or for an afternoon swim. If you were to anchor overnight, the length of the rode should be five to seven times the depth. In heavy weather you may want to pay out ten times the depth or more on two anchors. Consequently, the length of your anchor line should be about ten times the depth of water where you will anchor. If you normally anchor in 40 feet of water, you'll find it easiest to have two 200-foot coils of anchor line. Most of the time only one coil will be in use, but you'll have the spare for emergencies.

An anchor line can be all chain, all nylon, or a combination of both. The best anchor lines are those that have two to three fathoms (12 to 18 feet) of chain shackled directly to the anchor and a nylon anchor line shackled to the chain. The chain keeps the anchor as near to horizontal as possible, while the nylon line provides some resiliency to the anchor line. In heavy seas a nylon line allows the boat to pitch and heave at the end of the line without the restrictions imposed by a heavy anchor chain.

Each shackle should be moused—that is, a wire is passed through the shackle pin eye and wrapped around the shackle to prevent the pin from coming undone. See the table at right to decide on the ideal chain size for your boat. Mousing the pin will make it a little more difficult to get it around your windlass's chain gypsy, but it is safer in the long run. If your shackle pin comes undone, wave goodbye to your anchor.

STORM ANCHORS: RECOMMENDED SIZES			
Boat length ft (m)	Rode length ft (m)	Rode size in (mm)	Chain size* in (mm)
Up to 15 (4.6)	125 (38.1)	5/16 (8)	3/16 (5)
15 to 25 (4.6 to 7.6)	150 (45.7)	3/8 (10)	1/4 (6)
26 to 30 (7.9 to 9.1)	200 (61)	7/16 (11)	5/16 (8)
31 to 35 (9.4 to 10.6)	300 (91.4)	1/2 (13)	3/8 (10)
36 to 40 (10.9 to 12.1)	400 (121.9)	5/8 (16)	7/16 (11)
41 to 50 (12.5 to 15.2)	500 (152.4)	5/8 (16)	7/16 (11)
51 to 60 (15.5. to 18.3)	500 (152.4)	3/4 (18)	1/2 (12)

RECOMMENDED SIZES BY ANCHOR TYPE					
Boat length ft (m)	Fortress model no.	Plow lbs (kg)	Bruce lbs (kg)	Delta lbs (kg)	Danforth standard model
Up to 15 (4.6)	FX-7	6 (2.4)	4.4 (2)	9 (3.6)	8-S
15 to 25 (4.6 to 7.6)	FX-7	15 (6)	11 (5)	14 (5.7)	13-S
26 to 30 (7.9 to 9.1)	FX-11	25 (10.1)	16.5 (7.5)	22 (8.9)	22-S
31 to 35 (9.4 to 10.6)	FX-16	35 (14.1)	22 (10)	22 (8.9)	40-S
36 to 40 (10.9 to 12.1)	FX-23	45 (18.2)	33 (15)	35 (14.1)	65-S
41 to 50 (12.5 to 15.2)	FX-37	60 (24.2)	44 (20)	55 (22.2)	130-S
51 to 60 (15.5. to 18.3)	FX-55	75 (30.3)	66 (30)	55 (22.2)	180-S

*Recommended chain length: one-half foot of chain for each foot of boat length.
Larger vessels should use an all-chain rode.

▲ The sizes above are recommended by manufacturers as suitable for use as storm anchors. For everyday anchoring in good to moderate weather, one size smaller can be used in most cases. All uses assume good holding ground; a scope of at least five to one in good weather, more in storms; and shelter from prevailing seas.

Nylon is the most popular material for anchor line. It's strong, long-lasting, and relatively cheap. Most important, it's elastic, able to stretch from 15% to 25% of its original length. But make sure you buy marine-quality, three-strand nylon line rather than the less expensive, non-marine nylon, which will stiffen and become hard to use after it has been immersed in salt water for a while. Three-strand nylon anchor line is laid by twisting three separate strands of nylon together. The only problem with nylon is that because it stretches so much it is prone to chafe and must be protected.

Davis Instruments and Perimeter Industries both make chafe-guards that protect nylon anchor lines quite well. At the anchor end, chafe is prevented by splicing the nylon around a thimble through which the shackle is passed.

Another option is to buy braided Dacron line. This is not the double-braided line used for halyards, but a single braided line that stretches up to 20%, rather like a plaited line. The best braided anchor line is made by New England Ropes in Fall River, MA. Dacron is a very strong material and does not chafe quite as badly as nylon.

Polypropylene should not be used as an anchor line. It tends to float, which exerts an upward pull on the anchor.

Bow rollers

Another essential part of the anchor handling system is the bow roller. Anchor rollers help to keep the anchor away from the hull and serve as a place to stow the anchor. The best bow rollers are made to suit specific anchors and allow the anchor to be pinned tightly through the roller. Thus, the anchor is unlikely to go AWOL if the chain slips.

> To track the amount of scope you have out, **mark that scope!** Spend a few hours over the winter marking out your anchor line. You can either paint it at 1- or 2-fathom (6- or 12-feet) intervals up to 10 fathoms (60 feet). Then, at 5-fathom (30-feet) intervals you can splice brightly colored plastic markers through the anchor line.

A windlass has a horizontal axle and a capstan has a vertical axle, although the two names have become almost interchangeable. Windlasses and capstans should have a rope drum and a chain gypsy, as shown below. The rope drum is used to pull in the anchor line. The rope is then slid into the chain gypsy to secure the anchor tightly. This is a windlass for a larger boat, but many small boats use a low-profile windlass. The low-profile windlass poses special problems in that the nylon anchor line must be spliced right into the anchor chain so that it will go around the chain gypsy. Some low profile windlasses have a cut-out device to prevent the motor from overloading if undue strain is put on it. Sometimes this will happen when the anchor chain is only halfway in, and you will have either to haul it in by hand or to wait until the rest kicks in and the windlass works again.

▲ This vertical windlass has a smooth drum for line over a gypsy one for chain; they can be operated independently. The anchor chain passes around the gypsy and through a deck opening to the chain locker. The smooth drum can be used for a second anchor, or for warping the vessel into a berth.

Boathook

You'll need a boathook to pick up a mooring buoy or to grab a man-overboard life-ring tossed over the side when you practice your man overboard (MOB) drill.

Dock lines

You should have at least four dock lines. Two lines will be used as your bow and stern breast lines. You'll also need fore and aft springs to stop the boat surging forward or aft at the dock. Often, you'll be able to use the tails of the breast lines as spring lines to cut down on extra lines. If you are in an area where storms are likely, you should have additional dock lines to "double up" when the storm hits. All dock lines should be nylon to allow the boat to move around slightly after it is tied up.

▲ **An assortment of dock lines.**

Flags

You should carry the national flag on a staff on the stern of your boat. When you fly the flag, however, remember to take it down at sunset and hoist it again in the morning. If you belong to a boating club you can fly the club's burgee. If you want to dress ship—string flags from bow to stern—you'll need a full roll of flags.

Fishing gear

As long as you are on the water, why not have some fishing gear aboard? Take a rod or two, some lures, and learn the various fishing techniques. You may not catch much at first, but you will enjoy it anyway.

T-tops

If your boating will be in hot, sunny climates—and that's where the best boating is—you should have some form of shade over the helmsman. Many smaller boats have a T-top over the center console to provide shade. The T-top can also provide a location for radios and radar antenna.

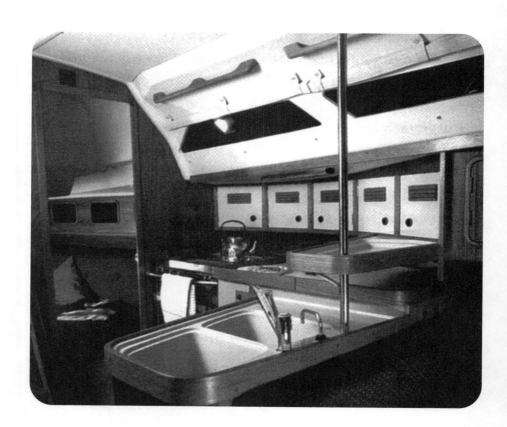

INSIDE
THE BOAT

I n this chapter, you will gain a greater understanding of the equipment that you find on board a boat. By knowing what gear belongs on a boat, how it is put together, and why one piece is better than another, you will be able to make good decisions about what you are looking at and what you want to do with it.

Below Deck

If you want to cook on your boat, you should have a well-planned galley. A galley for cooking on cruises will be very different from a galley on a boat used only for day trips. Day trips require nothing more than a portable ice chest for sandwiches and cold drinks. More elaborate meals require more sophisticated cooking and refrigeration facilities.

The galley: the heart of the boat

When comparing the galleys of similar boats, it's helpful to measure the amount of usable countertop space and the volume of the dry-storage compartments. Look for special touches such as slide-away cutting boards, a fold-out garbage pail, and slide-out food bins. These show that the builder has put extra thought into making the galley more efficient.

Here's a checklist of what to look for in a safe, workable galley.

- A location that removes the cook from the traffic pattern of the rest of the crew
- Anti-skid footing for the cook. If the galley doesn't have a good, non-slip floor, you can lay down a cork mat or other non-skid material.
- Handholds for the cook
- Places to put utensils and dishes while serving up meals
- A workable and secure arrangement for washing and drying dishes
- Drawers, doors, cupboards, and top-opening lockers that will stay secure in rough weather (no flying crockery or flatware)
- Adequate cutting-board space and countertop area for food preparation
- A stove large enough to accommodate your favorite dishes
- Adequate and accessible pot and pan stowage
- A stove with fiddle rails (3 to 4 inches) that will contain cookware and dishes when the boat rolls
- Adequate ventilation. At a minimum, there should be one opening port and one opening hatch close to the stove. Better yet, there should be Nicro battery- or solar-powered vents that can be fitted to the deck above the stove to vent the area continuously.

Space is at a premium in an onboard galley, and you will have to make do with far less storage space and fewer cooking utensils than in a regular kitchen. Although the galley is packed with cabinets and drawers, chances are that you will find that there are never enough of them and you will have to find additional places on the boat to store food.

For everyday use, cups and dishes can be plastic or paper, but many owners bring glass or china aboard. The shelves where you store your dishes should have partitions to keep them from banging together.

Stoves

The size and style of your stove depends upon the size of your boat. A small boat may have a portable, single-burner butane stove that can be used in the cockpit or below deck. Slightly larger boats will have a one- or two-burner electric stove that also may be fueled with alcohol. Larger boats may have a three- or four-burner stove powered by electricity with a separate oven and microwave. Many of today's stoves are ceramic with ribbon elements and heat-limiting surface protection. They can be cleaned simply by wiping them down and are stylish enough that many people buy similar units for their home.

Galley Maid makes several electric oven ranges for boats with two or three burners and an oven. These stoves drop right into a slot in the galley and are bolted in place. They are powered by either 110 or 220 volts of electricity, although propane units are also available. Propane is rarely used on a powerboat because it is heavier than air and the danger of an explosion is always present.

Electricity is probably the safest source of energy on board a boat, but shore power or an auxiliary generator—either on the engine or a separate generator—is required to produce the 110 or 220 volt AC power required. On larger boats power comes almost exclusively from a generator (sometimes called a genset), but on smaller boats the power may come from an engine-driven alternator. Or, the stove may be fueled with a combination of electricity and alcohol. On very small boats, a single-burner butane-powered stove may be used. For example, the self-igniting Kenyon model B2300 is fueled with an 8-ounce butane fuel cartridge that provides more than 7,000 BTUs of heat. This model can heat a quart of water in 6 minutes and provides up to 3 hours of cooking.

Microwaves

In recent years microwaves have provided an efficient alternative to the conventional stove. They reduce cooking time, power consumption, and the amount of heat released into the cabin. Microwave ovens can make time spent in the galley a far more pleasant experience for the crew on hot days. Most builders and owners install ordinary household microwaves on their boats. Although there are marine microwave ovens on the market, they are somewhat more expensive than the household units and may be slightly smaller. Twelve-volt microwaves are available but they are quite small—most measure about 9 square inches.

Inverter

If you wish to use your 110-volt microwave when the engine is turned off, you can use an inverter. An inverter turns 12- or 24-volt battery power into 110 volts to drive household appliances such as TVs or hairdryers. Inverters should use high power for a short time or low power for a longer time. They should not use high power for a long time as it will drain the batteries completely.

⚓ T I P

Install ground fault circuit interrupters (GFCIs) into your electrical systems to ground random electrical currents before they find another conductor —like you.

Refrigeration

Boat owners who plan to entertain a lot or take a boat out for long day or multi-day cruises opt for the convenience of mechanical refrigeration—usually an electric-motor compressor. These marine units use a non-toxic and non-flammable refrigerant, non-sparking motors, safety valves on high-pressure portions of the system, and construction designed to survive the rigors of marine service. Such refrigeration units are reliable and long-lasting. They can last for years, even with continuous use.

Usually 3 to 6 cubic feet, the units operate either from the 12-volt DC power of the onboard alternator and battery bank or 110-volt AC power generated from the engine alternator, or from shore power. Usually the refrigerator shares battery power with electric lights, water pumps, and heater and van fans. Many boats use a Norcold refrigerator/freezer that fits under the galley counter. On larger boats, commercial-sized refrigerators and freezers may be used.

The marine toilet or "the head"

A marine bathroom is usually called a head. The marine toilet is an important part of the accommodations of any boat. Even boats without a cabin often have a small compartment for a marine toilet. The head area should also include a sink and a drawer for first-aid supplies. On these small boats, the toilet may only be a Porta Potti or similar unit that you take ashore and empty after your day or weekend trip is finished. On larger boats the toilet is built in and must empty into a holding tank. No wastes can be discharged over the side in areas such as Narragansett Bay, RI. You must visit the pump-out stations to discharge the contents of your holding tank. Other areas of the country are also adopting no-discharge policies.

⚓ **T I P**
On small boats, try a portable marine head—or Porta Potti.

Larger boats may have a Lectrasan unit that uses electricity to cremate effluent and render it into ash. There is some discussion of whether the ash can be discharged, but currently it, too, must go into a holding tank. Very large vessels have black water (giant holding) tanks that hold the effluent until it can be discharged ashore or at sea. The latest marine toilets are completely self-contained, electric-powered, flushable toilets that macerate and dispose of sewage directly into the holding tank.

⚓ **T I P**
Clean the head after each trip with a commercial toilet cleaner.

The shower

Small boats under 24 feet generally do not have a shower. If you need one onboard, use the saltwater washdown pump or a bucket of seawater. Large boats up to 35 feet usually have a combined toilet/shower compartment that is only used when the family stays aboard for a weekend or longer. Only the largest boats have a separate shower compartment. On these boats the toilet and shower spaces should each be at least 28 inches wide, although a 32- to 36-inch shower is more comfortable. Above the shower there should be some form of ventilator to suck the humidity from the shower out of the boat.

⚓ **T I P**
Keep a bar of seawater soap aboard, just in case.

Bunks should be at least 6 feet 4 inches long and about 28 to 30 inches wide. In hot weather, the largest bunk seems too small, but in a storm you'll want the smallest bunk possible to keep you wedged in place.

In the forward part of many boats are the vee-berths. In most cases, these bunks are only usable in harbor. The pitching motion of the boat as it moves through the waves makes them untenable in anything other than the calmest seas. If you plan to accomodate two people in the vee berth, try before you buy. Quite often vee berths measure 6 feet or less on the diagonal and may be smaller from top to bottom.

Settee berths

In the dinette, or sitting area, the settees can often be converted into a bunk. In this case, the seat needs only to be about 18 inches deep, but a bunk should be at least 28 inches wide. To make the bunk wider than the sofa seat, manufacturers resort to a number of methods. They may make the area behind the seat back open to allow you to stow a pillow and bedding behind it. When it comes time to turn in, the seatback is removed and the bedding pulled out on an adequately wide seat. Other manufacturers install a seat back that can be removed and dropped into place alongside the seat. Still others offer a transom or drawer-like pull-out berth that does the job. There are any number of strategies. You should make sure that the method used on your boat is adequate, as some bunks have been known to collapse.

Storage space

Boats need to have lots of storage space. When you go aboard for the first time, you will probably bring casual clothes, sandals or boat shoes, towels, and loads of other equipment. All these items will need to be stowed. Unless your boat is over about 40 feet, you will not have enough space to stow everything and will have to compromise. For example, on a 24-footer with three or four crew, sleeping overnight often entails tossing everyone's seabag into the nearest open floor space to ensure that all the crew have a bunk. The next day, the bunks are filled with seabags while the crew sails.

In the galley, you'll want to stow food. If space is at a premium, the cook may use unusual spaces elsewhere. For example, canned goods get stowed in the bilge. For a long trip, extra bread may be stowed in all manner of places, even the head. In general, stow heavy stuff low and light stuff high to increase the boat's stability.

TIP

If stowing canned goods in the bilge, remove paper labels and use a magic marker to name the contents. Paper labels rot and drop off.

Ventilation

Ventilation should be adequate throughout the boat without the need to open hatches. A boat that is left at the marina or dock for a week should have some method of automatically circulating air throughout the hull. Usually this means several vents on the side of the cabin or on the cabin top. Circulating air keeps the boat smelling fresh and helps to prevent mildew. If the boat is locked up tight all week, you will find that stale odors, mildew, and rot will start fairly quickly. During bright sunny days the interior temperature of your boat may routinely exceed a hundred and twenty degrees. If you leave food or drinks onboard, high temperatures will probably spoil them.

CHAPTER 9

NAVIGATION AND ELECTRONIC AIDS

N ot only do boaters need to know how to use a chart, but they also need to know how to use electronic instruments. While charts should always be on board your boat, you may also have a radar, a plotter, a Global Positioning System, and an autopilot, all of which may be linked together to enable the flow of information between them. Using electronics, you can also keep in touch with friends and family, explore the Internet, navigate, and tell people where you are while you are in the middle of the ocean.

The old-fashioned, tried-and-true hand navigation tools are a must, and you should know how to use them. A compass that has been adjusted properly, charts, parallel rules, and a sharp pencil will get you to most harbors safely and quickly. A book of tide and current tables, a hand bearing compass, and keen eye will be all that you require on most trips. You should learn to navigate using these old-fashioned methods before you invest in electronic equipment.

TIP

For waterway guides and chart kits for specific areas, call the Better Boating Association (781-982-4060); Waterway Guides (770-955-2500); or Embassy Boating Guides (888-839-5551).

Compass and Charts

The most essential tool on any powerboat is still a compass. A compass determines direction by means of a freely rotating needle indicating magnetic north. A compass card, labeled with geographic directions, is mounted inside the compass. Your compass should be mounted directly on the pedestal or within easy sight of the helmsman. The lubber line—a dark line on the compass dome—should be aligned with the fore and aft centerline of the boat.

The markings on the cards should be large and simple enough to be read in bad weather and through spray or mist. The compass should have a dimmable red light to make it easy to read at night. The larger the compass, the easier it will be to read (and the more expensive it will probably be). A compass and charts are still required equipment aboard every boat, and no experienced boater would go to sea without studying a chart first. American charts are made by the U.S. National Oceanic and Atmospheric Administration (NOAA). Charts for other countries are made by their hydrographic offices.

> Make sure that you **swing the boat's compass** as soon as you take possession of it. If the compass was swung by the previous owner and you have moved the boat to a new area, have it swung properly. The earth's magnetic field is not consistent from coast to coast. An inaccurate compass can take you miles off course, and in fog you might go aground rather than into the harbor.

They show water depth, the shape of land masses, latitude and longitude, and the location of navigational markers. For NOAA Charts, US Chart 1 shows what each symbol represents.

It is important to note that while your compass will point to magnetic north, the chart will indicate geographic north. That's because magnetic north is not true north on most points on the globe. The difference between the two is called variation. There is as much as 20 degrees variation along the northern coasts of Maine and Washington. If you are traveling long distances and navigating by compass, you will want to know how many degrees you should add to or subtract from your course to compensate for the extent of variation in a given area.

> **TIP**
> Don't look at the compass all the time as you steer a "compass course." Get your directional bearing and then steer toward a land-mark straight ahead.

COMPASS CRITERIA

When shopping for a compass, choose a quality instrument. Consider the points listed below. Remember that your compass is the most important navigational tool aboard your boat. **This is no place to cut corners.**

1. Can the compass be mounted in a location on your boat that allows for comfortable viewing for long periods of time?

2. Is the card easily read and appropriately marked?

3. Does the card remain level? It should not stick through reasonable levels of pitch and roll.

4. Does the card move uniformly through any course change?

5. Is the card "dead-beat?" That is, does it swing only once to a steady position?

6. Are there built-in compensating magnets?

7. Is there provision for night lighting, preferably with a dimmer?

8. Is the dome hemispherically shaped rather than flat?

9. Are the card and lubber's line fully gimbaled? Internal gimbals are best.

10. Is there a metal or rubber expansion chamber to allow for temperature changes?

11. Is there any significant parallax error when the compass is viewed from the side as compared to the rear?

LORAN

For about 50 years, Long Range Navigation System (LORAN) was the prime electronic navigation system for the United States and Canada. The Global Positioning System (GPS) has replaced it as the system of choice. But if you buy an older boat, you may find it still equipped with LORAN. In fact, many anglers prefer it for its repeatable accuracy. LORAN utilizes a network of shore-based radio transmitters that are grouped in "chains." These chains are designed to provide accurate navigational fixes within 50 nautical miles from shore or out to the 100-fathom curve, whichever is greater. The U.S. government, which has maintained the system, is gradually phasing it out. Chances are that it will be completely replaced by the GPS within the next two decades.

The Global Positioning System (GPS)

The Global Positioning System is an advanced worldwide navigation system designed and operated by the U.S. Department of Defense. It relies on signals transmitted from a group of 24 orbiting satellites. A GPS receiver determines vessel position by taking virtually instantaneous readings from at least three satellites. The position of each satellite becomes the radius of a sphere. The receiver calculates the vessel's position as the point at which the three spheres intersect. It can tell you the speed, course, latitude, and longitude of your boat.

GPS units

GPS units come in either shelf-mounted or portable handheld models. They are relatively inexpensive and getting cheaper all the time. The latest GPS units are 12 channel receivers—that is, they can pick up 12 satellites at once and use the best signals to get an accurate fix on a boat's location. Shelf-mounted units cost upwards of $200 depending on the features, and portable units run as little as $89.

The latest GPS units can display buoys, cities, and streets, and can be used for navigation on board your boat or to get you home overland after your boating trip. To increase the repeatable accuracy of GPS, many manufacturers are adding in a feature known as Differential GPS (DGPS). DGPS uses radio waves in a manner similar to LORAN, and uses them to increase the accuracy of the GPS location. While Differential was originally used to replace the government installed Selective Availability (SA), it has come into its own now that SA has been turned off.

Chart plotters

A chart plotter shows a chart of the area in which you are boating and locates your boat on that chart by means of the GPS signal. Chart plotters can be mounted in the cockpit, and some are available with daylight-viewable screens. (In the past the biggest problem with plotters has been that the LCD screen "disappears" in bright sunlight.) Some daylight-viewable screens are about the size of a laptop computer screen and can be used to plot your course before you set out. When you have plotted your course, you can link the plotter to the autopilot and, in theory, the boat will sail to its destination. When this system is linked to wind instruments in a complete system, such as the one available from RayMarine, the boat can sail to windward on autopilot.

Chart plotters are one of the most popular electronic gizmos ever to come along. With a chart plotter installed at your helm station, you can see your boat's track on the screen as it moves along. Before you go on your trip you can lay out a course, store waypoints, and calculate how far it is to your destination, and how long it will take you to get there. When you start on your trip you can plug in the autopilot and have the autopilot/GPS/plotter combination take you to your destination. Chart plotters can use an internal or external GPS input, display buoys, charts, navaids, and city streets, and some (depending on the software used) can tell you where the local chandlery or restaurants are when you come to a port.

Depth finders

Depth finders (also known as Fathometers) use an echo-ranging pulse to determine the distance between the hull of your boat and the sea bottom. They will help keep you out of shallow water and can also help you determine your position in a dense fog by enabling you to compare the depth on the finder with the depth recorded on the chart. The most inexpensive units, digital depth finders, show the depth in numbers displayed on a screen. Most popular, however, are the LCD screen displays, which show the bottom of the sea visually, including the fish swimming beneath the boat. LCD displays are invaluable to anglers, and a source of delight to kids.

Fish finders

If you are a truly dedicated fisherman, you might want to look into a colored fish finder. These daylight-visible, colored LCD display screens show the contours of the seabed and also show any fish that get between the fish finder and the seabed. Generally, the fish shows up as a different color on the screen. Companies such as RayMarine make fish finders that can be linked to your DGPS to bring you back to the same area every time.

Radar

Radar has a unique advantage in navigation in that a single instrument can measure both direction and distance to objects. Radar can almost always make a measurement of direction despite fog, light rain, or darkness. Even small boats can have some of the latest LCD display radar sets. The latest radars integrate GPS location and have overlays of charts to enable the user to tell exactly where the boat is in relation to charts and to the shoreline.

Even more than other piloting methods, radar requires considerable practice and experience. Develop your radar skills during fair weather and good conditions so that they are readily available in difficult circumstances and you can use them with confidence.

Electronic charts are the most important part of plotter and GPS displays. There are a number of electronic chart manufacturers, but the only ones used in plotters are vector charts made by C-Map or Navionics.

Understanding electronic charts

There are two types of electronic charts: raster and vector. Raster charts are paper charts that have been scanned into a computer. By adjusting for scale and data, most of the electronic chart programs seamlessly integrate raster charts into one master chart. With raster charts you see the same amount of detail whether you have zoomed in or out to the maximum.

Vector charts, on the other hand, are raster charts that have been reprogrammed so that each depth (or height) contour and each set of Navaids, etc., are on different layers of the chart. This means that if you zoom out to the largest scale you will see outlines of continents and a few depth contours. As you keep zooming in, more detail reveals itself, until you can see each slip in a marina. Vector charts often incorporate more details than can be found on raster charts. For instance, some charts have a database of marinas, restaurants, repair shops and other pertinent information that can be turned on or off at will.

Don't confuse electronic charts with navigation programs. Electronic charts allow you to do exactly what you do with a paper chart without a pencil or parallel rules. Electronic navigation programs allow you to utilize electronic charts in the same way a pencil, parallel rules, and a compass allow you to use a paper chart. Over and above that, electronic charts have some extra features. For example, instead of looking up tide tables, you can turn on the tide table overlay and see the tide arrows. If you animate the sequence you can watch the tide change over the course of your trip.

To use an electronic navigation program, first zoom out until you can see your starting point and destination. Plot your course from one way point to the other without worrying if you cut across a bit of land. Now zoom in and add waypoints to insert the details of your course. Make sure that you go around the hard stuff, leaving plenty of water around reefs, wrecks, and other shallow spots. Once the course information has been input (you can do this in an evening on your home computer) you can check the tide situation against your departure time, modify it if necessary, and save the entire program. For example, if you are leaving Long Island Sound's eastern end, you must go through one of three exits, Fisher's Island Sound, The Race, or The Gut. As the tide roars through these places at up to 6 knots, you need to plan your trip so that you will arrive at The Race or The Gut when the tide is going with you. To figure this out manually can be a tedious process, but by using an electronic chart program, you can do it in a few minutes.

On an electronic chart program you can also project where your boat will be in 5 or ten minutes, put a "hazard" ring around the boat—if the ring touches a hazard such as a wreck buoy, it sounds an alarm—or turn on or off the depth arrows so you know what depth of water you are sailing in. With the very latest programs you can access the program maker's website, download weather information for your area, and get up-to-the-minute information on wind direction and strength.

Wherever you are on the water, you will want to be able to contact the rest of the world. Maybe you want to find out what a cloud buildup portends, or let someone know where you are, or find out if someone will meet the boat when you arrive. If you're within 20 miles of land, a cell phone is the most convenient way to contact other people, but you have to remember to keep the phone charged. However, you should not use a cell phone to call for help or assistance unless you have no other method. The U.S. Coast Guard (USCG) cannot determine where the call originates. A cell phone signal might be relayed through a satellite dish in New Jersey while you are in Maine. Consequently, the USCG cannot triangulate where you are if you are not able to give a precise location.

Very High Frequency (VHF) radio

At longer distances with ranges up to 30 miles, depending on the height of the antenna, the top communications gear is VHF radio. The transmissions are basically line-of-sight, so if you are low down in a dinghy, you may only have a range of three miles. VHF signals are not reflected by the atmosphere, nor do they bend around the curvature of the earth.

The most important use of the VHF radio is safety. Anyone who has a radio turned on is required by law to monitor Channel 16 when not actually engaged on another channel. Channel 16 is the only channel to be used for distress calls and messages. It is the channel you would use if it were ever necessary to broadcast the Mayday call, signaling the danger of loss of life or vessel. The USCG also monitors this channel. Channel 16 is also used to establish contact with other boats, but only in order to agree on which working channel you will switch to. No non-emergency transmission on Channel 16 may exceed 30 seconds.

In order to lessen the congestion on Channel 16, the Federal Communications Commission has authorized the voluntary use of Channel 09 by non-commercial vessels for calling each other. Maintaining a watch for calls on Channel 09, however, may result in missing warnings and announcements from USCG stations and Marine Operators.

TIP

Safety first: while at sea, keep your VHF radio tuned to Channel 16!

VHF

In order to minimize transmission time, VHF calls follow a standard operating procedure. A typical conversation would proceed as follows:

"Happy Day. . .Happy Day, this is Red Bird, over."

"Red Bird, this is Happy Day."

"Happy Day, this is Red Bird. Switch six-eight."

"Roger, Red Bird. This is Happy Day. Roger six-eight."

Both stations retune to Channel 68.

At the end of the call:

"Happy Day, out."

"Red Bird, out."

Console-mounted VHF radios cost about $160 to $500. So does the handheld VHF, which is approximately the same size as a cell phone. Portable units are useful as a backup for a regular radio and in small boats with no installed radio system. However, they have limited output power and their antennas are much shorter and less efficient than those on other radios. As a result, they are unsuitable for anything more than relatively close communication.

> ⚓ **T I P**
> One great thing about VHF: it's free once you buy the equipment.

For distances longer than 25 or 30 miles, single side-band (SSB) radio transmitters are used. SSBs send signals to relaying communication satellites. A vessel cannot be licensed for an SSB radiotelephone unless it is already equipped with a VHF set, and the skipper is required to try to communicate via VHF before using the lower and crowded frequencies of the SSB. Installation of SSB equipment usually requires the services of a trained and licensed technician. Unlike VHF radio, SSB requires a large "ground plane" of copper mesh panel in order to radiate its signals, and the panel must be installed professionally.

EPIRB

Every boat that goes offshore beyond reliable VHF radio range—roughly 20 miles—should carry an Emergency Position Indicating Radio Beacon (EPIRB). First-generation EPIRBs, operating on the 121.5 Mhz band and divided into Class A and Class B, operate on the emergency channels for civilian planes and the "guard" channel for military aircraft. When one or more of these detect the tone signal of an EPIRB, search and rescue activities begin. Unfortunately, first-generation EPIRBs suffer from voice-communication interference and the units have a very high incidence of false alarms. By some counts, over 90% of calls are false alarms.

Much more reliable are the second-generation EPIRBs that operate on the 406.5 Mhz band, and use a dedicated frequency free of interference from other communications. Beacon signals are picked up by orbiting satellites. At $800 to $1,400, they are considerably more expensive than the first-generation equipment, but their far greater effectiveness makes the cost worthwhile. Some units can be interfaced to a GPS receiver and locate the distress location to less than a half mile. At close to $2,000, they are even more expensive.

The latest development in EPIRB technology is to link the EPIRB to a GPS unit. This unit transmits the GPS location of the unit and can cut rescue time to a matter of minutes instead of hours or days. Once any EPIRB is activated in an emergency, it must be left on. To turn it off "to save the battery" severely disrupts rescue operations.

CHAPTER 10

BE PREPARED

A s skipper, you are responsible for the well-being of your boat and of everyone on board. You need to be as self-sufficient as possible on the water, which means having everything from tool and first-aid kits to life rafts.

Basic boat care is an ongoing proposition. There are repairs for which you will need an expert repairperson. But while you're at sea, that's your job description.

Keeping a toolbox at sea is a special challenge. Even if the tools don't get wet, they are liable to rust in the salt air and spray. Store them in a watertight kit and store the kit in a dry-storage box. Then, every time you use a tool, rub it clean with an oiled rag to prevent corrosion. Or you can spend a little extra and get a non-corroding tool kit.

Here are some of the most basic, must-have tools:

- Two pairs of locking pliers: a 5-inch and a 9-inch
- Adjustable wrench
- Prop nut wrench
- Slip-joint and needle-nosed pliers
- Flat screwdrivers, including one with an extra-long shaft for those hard-to-reach places
- Phillips-head screwdrivers
- Set of hex keys
- Vise grips
- Sockets
- Claw hammer
- C-clamps
- Small brushes
- Hand drill and bits
- Torque wrench for adjusting bolts
- Electrical pliers
- Last, but not least, magnetic "wand" for retrieving bolts and other small tools that fall into the bilge.

TIP

Is your engine too noisy? Insulate it by adding foam sheets to the inside of your engine box.

Leaks and tears

You'll need an assortment of items to help patch holes and control leaks. Duct tape has a million uses, from fixing a hose to sealing a bag. Marine sealer and super glue will help you stick just about anything together. For your engines, you might want to keep around some epoxy-resin-based auto-body filler for temporary repairs.

If your boat starts to leak, it's probably because of damage to through-hull fittings and related parts such as hoses and keel bolts. Have on board softwood plugs and make sure you have one of appropriate diameter for each size of through-hull fitting on your boat. You can drive the plugs into place from the inside. Also keep on board underwater epoxy putty and rags for stuffing in cracks.

You'll also need an assortment of spare parts. Don't bring gear you'll never use, but go through your onboard equipment and bring spare kits for pumps and compressors, hoses, clamps, belts, and, if you know how to use them, spare gaskets for the main engines. Some people who go up to 40 miles offshore and know about these things bring a spare injector for a diesel, but you have no need for that if you go from one inshore port to another.

Other items in your spare parts kit should include: nuts, bolts, screws, washers of the sizes that fit most of your engines or pumps, extra fuses, insulating electrical tape, insulated wire, stainless steel hose clamps, a small copper or brass wire brush, one or two plastic buckets, extra batteries, nylon tie-wraps, and some stiff wire such as coat hangers to retrieve tools or parts from behind the gas tank or from the bilge. Swiss army knives are always useful, as are the popular multi-tools available from most hardware stores.

TIP
Make sure that you always have spare batteries for all your flashlights.

Finally, the most important tool you'll need if you go out after dark is a flashlight, or rather, several flashlights, because you can never have too many. Whether you're down in the engine room in the morning or up on deck at night, you'll need a waterproof flashlight. Get different types—a rechargeable one or two, a wide beam light for illuminating areas after you have dropped something, a narrow beam light or two for concentrated light, and a large spotlight for coming into a harbor at night. You can also have spotlights installed on most powerboats, either fitted on the bridge or on the bow.

You should always carry enough gear so that you'll be able to get your motor going even if it breaks down far from shore. This requires specific spare parts and, especially if you have an outboard motor, extra oil.

TIP

Just in case your motor won't start and you're close to shore, stock a paddle. On smaller boats, it might come in handy.

Two-cycle outboard engines take between 20 to 40 parts gasoline to 1 part of oil. You should always keep at least one extra gallon container of TCW-3 oil handy, so that you can fill the oil injection reservoir if it runs dry. Keep a plastic funnel handy to get the oil into the tank. You can make one from a 1-quart oil container. You don't want to run out of oil, because running an outboard without oil will destroy the engine.

Inboard engines, whether gasoline or diesel, burn little oil with their fuel. Therefore, you don't need to keep as much of it on board. Keep a quart of oil on board for an inboard gasoline engine, and 4 quarts for a diesel. Diesels require oil more often than gasoline engines. And don't forget the funnel. You should also keep some coolant for your engine's cooling system.

TIP

Carry spare fuel filters on board. In high seas, sediment in the fuel tanks can get stirred up and may clog fuel filters. If you don't know how, ask your local mechanic to show you how to change a fuel filter.

Older inboard and outboard gas engines require spare spark plugs and a spark plug wrench, spare propeller, prop nut, washer, cotter pin, and shear pin. On small outboard motors, bring a starter rope in case the battery dies. On inboards, bring spare fuel filter elements, hydraulic fuel, shaft packing, point file, gaskets, and spare drive belts.

Although a deep suntan was once considered fashionable or healthy, today's medical recommendations warn about the dangers of chronic overexposure to the sun. Medical research shows that too much ultraviolet radiation not only causes skin to age prematurely, but may cause skin cancer to develop. Since boating involves hours on end in the sun, you can minimize your risk by taking the following precautions and by stocking your boat with the following:

✔ Protect your skin with good-quality commercial sunscreen that protects from both ultraviolet alpha (UVA) and ultraviolet beta (UVB) rays. The American Academy of Dermatology recommends year-round sun protection for everyone, and especially for fair-skinned people and those who burn easily. The Food and Drug Administration recognizes Sun Protection Factor (SPF) values between 2 and 15. It has not been determined whether sunscreens with SPF ratings over 15 provide additional protection.

> **TIP**
> Remember: even on cloudy days, water, sand, and other surfaces reflect light that can burn severely.

✔ Apply sunscreen 15 to 30 minutes before exposure to the sun, and reapply often (every 60 to 90 minutes). Have a stash of sunscreen onboard as you'll go through a lot of it. **Kids on board?** Be sure to carry sunscreen made especially for children, whose skin is usually quite sensitive. **Swimmers** should use sunscreens labeled "water-resistant" and reapply as prescribed on the label.

✔ Wear UV blocking, wrap-around sunglasses. According to the American Red Cross, opthalmologists recommend sunglasses that have a UV absorption rate of 90% or above. Attach holders to your sunglasses, such as those made by Croakies or Chum's, to keep your sunglasses on. Also attach a "floater" to your glasses, just in case they do fall off in the water. Ask your eye doctor if you need prescription sunglasses.

✔ Exposure to the sun between the hours of 10 AM and 2 PM is the most harmful. Select clothing that minimizes your exposure to the sun, such as a wide-brimmed hat or visor, long-sleeved shirts, and long pants.

First-aid kit

On shore, emergency medical assistance is usually just minutes away. But on the water, you may be on your own for quite a while before help comes. Your confidence and competence in handling medical emergencies should be on a par with your seamanship skills. That confidence comes from knowledge and practice; both can be acquired and honed by basic and advanced first-aid courses.

In addition to at least one comprehensive first-aid manual, your boat should be equipped with a first-aid kit designed specifically for your needs. Day and weekend boaters, for example, need a kit stocked with basics such as:

- ► Thermometer
- ► Gauze
- ► Aspirin
- ► Antibiotic cream or gel
- ► Tweezers
- ► Alcohol

- ► Sunscreen
- ► Bandages (plastic and cloth, assorted sizes)
- ► Scissors
- ► Eye-washing cup
- ► Hot water bottle/ice bag

Depending on the cruising waters and the crew members aboard, you might also want to stock items such as remedies for seasickness and jellyfish stings.

Long-range cruisers require more extensive first-aid supplies and lifesaving equipment, as well as a wide range of medications. In order to reduce the caregiver's risk of infection, every first-aid kit should also include a waterless antiseptic hand cleaner and disposable gloves.

TIP

Make sure you bring along any prescription medicines that you may require, especially if you are going away for the weekend.

Life rafts

Any boat that operates more than a few miles offshore should be equipped with a Safety of Life at Sea- (SOLAS-) approved life raft with the following features: canister stowage for greater long-term protection, automatic inflation, insulated floor, a canopy, boarding ladder and lifelines, a painter, locator lights, a survival and first-aid kit, a rainwater collector, a drogue or sea anchor, an Emergency Position Indicating Radio Beacon (ERIRB), and other signaling devices. The raft should accommodate the largest number of people likely to be aboard while the boat is offshore.

When purchasing a life raft, remember that an eight-man raft has room for eight people sitting down, not lying down. Life rafts are very hard to get into from the water, and the old adage—step up into the life raft—should be taken seriously. According to life raft manufacturers, the first thing that will happen when you get into a raft is that you will get seasick, so prepare for it.

Life rafts are cumbersome, expensive to purchase, and require expensive annual inspections. But if you go out of sight of land you should have one. It could mean the difference between a mishap and a disaster.

▲ **Make sure a life raft is part of your "survival kit."**

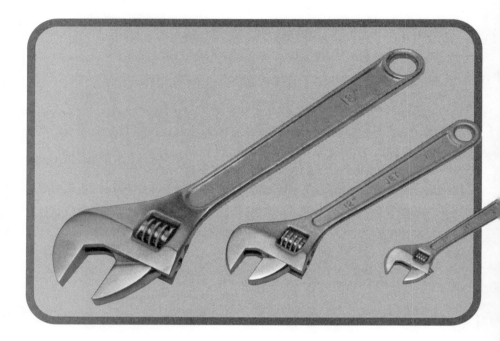

PART III

MAINTENANCE

B oats, like any machines, need to be maintained or the bits and pieces eventually break. Some maintenance should be done on a weekly or even daily basis; other work can be done once or twice a year. Good maintenance can help keep the resale value of your boat high. Poor maintenance will drop its resale value by more than the cost of the maintenance. What you do is up to you, but you will enjoy your boat more if it is in tip-top shape.

CHAPTER 11

CARING FOR YOUR BOAT

To keep your boat functioning smoothly while you own it and maximize its resale value, it is best to follow a list of procedures during each trip and maintain all of the systems required to run the boat. Use the guidelines in this chapter to custom-design a checklist for your particular boat. Keep a record in the boat's log of all inspections, tests, and servicing of fire extinguishers.

MAINTENANCE CHECKLIST

Before your trip:

► Check the battery.

► Put in the bilge drain plug.

► Ventilate the engine bilge.

► Inspect all safety gear.

► Turn on the electronic equipment to make sure it works.

► Examine the engine and fuel system for cleanliness and leaks.

► Wipe up any oil or grease drippings and do not use the boat until any leaks are fixed.

► Stow all gear safely.

After your return:

► Hose down the boat, motor, and trailer with fresh water.

► Clean the interior of the boat.

► Remove the bilge drain plug (unless you leave the boat in the water).

► Turn the battery off.

► Inspect the propeller, if you haul the boat.

Once or twice a season:

► Inspect lifesaving equipment. Replace sub-standard lifesaving devices immediately.

► Check portable and installed fire-extinguishing systems.

► Lubricate all grease points on the motor and trailer.

► Scrub the hull.

► Polish and protect all stainless steel fittings and rails.

► Treat all vinyl and canvas with a preservative to prevent cracking and mildew.

► Spray exposed electrical connections with electrical contact cleaner.

► Check the lower unit gearcase oil.

► Lubricate hinges and canvas snaps.

- Check belts and hoses.
- Check battery fluid level or levels.
- Check all lighting for bad bulbs, connections, etc.
- Check through-hull fittings for a proper seal.
- Check drain hoses and clamps.

At the end of every season (or at least once a year if you keep your boat in the water year-round):

- Haul the boat out of the water for bottom cleaning and repainting. Have the yard pressure-wash the hull.
- Inspect hull and fittings below waterline—shafts, propellers, rudders, struts, stuffing boxes, and metal skegs.
- Check the engine tune.
- Change the lower unit oil.
- Change fuel/water separator.
- Replace water pump impeller.
- Replace zincs.
- Check the entire fuel system inch by inch, including fuel lines in areas not normally visible. When replacing fuel system components, use equivalent replacement parts rather than automotive parts. If any joints or lengths of tubing or hose are worn or damaged, call a qualified mechanic without delay.
- Have a qualified professional inspect the electrical system.
- Disconnect storage batteries if you are leaving the boat out of the water for the winter. Bring the batteries home and keep them fully charged with a trickle charger once per month.
- Discharge the fire extinguisher to test it.
- Discharge one of the portable fire-extinguishing units each year on a regular basis—preferably as a drill with all crew members participating. On shore, put out a small fire in a metal pan or tub. Then have the extinguisher serviced and reinstalled as soon as possible.

The bottom isn't as easy to get to and clean as the rest of your boat. But it is most important to clean because barnacles and algae can ruin the surface of your hull in a matter of weeks. In freshwater, algae and zebra mussels pose the most problems and will be the most stubborn life forms to attach to your boat. In salt water, the enemy is slime, which allows weeds to grow, providing a habitat for barnacles.

You should use a good-quality bottom paint if you keep your boat in the water. Bottom paints come in several types. Slime-fighter paints with a biocide, such as Interlux's latest two-part Micron Optima bottom paint, stop the slime from growing on your boat. If you can stop slime from growing, the barnacles do not have a medium for their eggs to grip onto. If you moor your boat in waters that are heavily brackish—that is, a mixture of salt and fresh water—you should use a paint with the latest combination of biocides. For example, not only does Optima contain copper oxide, but it also has zinc pyridinethione and a unique slime-fighting ingredient to really keep your boat's hull clean. If your boat is moored in an area where weeds grow quickly, such as a Floridia estuary, get a paint with a high copper content, such as Ultra Kote, which is 76% copper biocide.

If you buy a new boat, your first step should be to apply a bottom-protecting paint so that you will never have an osmosis problem. Interlux's Interprotect can be applied after scrubbing the fiberglass surface of a new boat with soap and water. Then just follow the instructions on the can. In a survey done by International Paint it was found that a boat with a bottom protected by Interprotect sold for an average of $877 per gallon of paint more than one with an unprotected bottom. In other words, if your 18-foot runabout uses two gallons of paint (costing about $60 to $70 per gallon), the resale value of your boat could be about $1600 more than that of an unprotected boat.

After applying Interprotect, you apply the bottom paint. Choose the bottom paint that is most suitable for your boat and style of boating. If you have a trawler-style yacht you can use a conventional "soft"—that is, a less expensive rosin-based bottom paint. Or you can use an ablative paint (one in which the outer paint erodes away, exposing new biocide as it erodes) if you use your boat a lot. If your boat has a good turn of speed you should use a "hard" bottom paint, such as Super Fiberglass BottomKote. This paint has a 57% copper content and is specially formulated for powerboats. It can be applied up to 60 days before launching without losing effectiveness.

If you use your boat on weekends and trailer it to and from your boating area, you do not really need a bottom paint. But if you decide to use one, you should get a multi-use paint that allows you to launch and retrieve your boat without the paint becoming less functional when it is out of the water.

TIP
Bleach will take care of that dirty green line on your hull.

Aluminum boats should not be coated with copper-based paints, because this will turn a boat into a large battery and could cause major damage. Aluminum boats should be coated with special aluminum paint such as Tri-Lux II. Or you can try the new Veridian paint.

Veridian is a silicone bottom paint with no antifouling properties at all. It is so slippery that barnacles simply slide off when the boat runs at speed. However, if you decide to use this paint, you need to run your boat frequently (at least once a week) to make sure the "clingons" slide off. You can also use Tri-Lux II or Veridian on your lower unit to keep it clean and unfouled. Note that Tri-Lux II does not contain Tributyltin, which has been almost completely banned because of environmental concerns.

One of the reasons fiberglass boats are so popular is that they're so easy to repair. If there is a scratch in the hull, you can fix it yourself. To repair minor scrapes and scratches, use a two-part gel coat (if your boat is white). Mix the gel coat and use a plastic spatula to fill the scratch. If the damage is a little more severe, take some two-part epoxy resin such as MAS, WEST, System 3, or Epiglass, and mix it with a filler such as lightweight fairing compound, and spread it over small holes up to about one-half inch in diameter.

Do not attempt large repairs unless you have had some experience using fiberglass and epoxy. Fiberglass and resins can make a horrendous mess. If you make a mistake, the only thing to do is wipe off what you can, come back with a grinder when everything has set, and grind the mess away. By the way, grinding fiberglass is probably the most miserable job you'll ever want to try. Wear a Tyvek suit with elastic bands over the cuffs and ankles, a respirator, goggles, and gloves to grind fiberglass or you will itch for days. Having said that, here's how you do it:

Large holes or dents that go through the hull laminate will need to be ground back and some form of backing put in place to stop the fiberglass collapsing. Fiberglass cloth is just like the fabric in your shirt only a little thicker. If you try to stand fiberglass on edge it will collapse just like a shirt would. With a support (such as a layer of masonite covered with polyethylene plastic or mold release wax) in place on the inside of the hole, a layer of fiberglass is cut to fit and wetted out using previously mixed epoxy resin with no fillers. (Wet out by pouring a little resin onto the fiberglass cloth and rolling it with a metal roller. Don't roll too hard or you will introduce air bubbles into the laminate.) Keep applying fiberglass layers and wetting them out until you have built up a suitable thickness (equal to the previous hull thickness). Then let the whole mess set. Allow at least 24 hours for the epoxy to dry and become sandable, then grind or sand it smooth. You may have to fill any slight holes or recesses with fairing compound until you get the entire thing perfectly smooth. Ideally, you should finish up with 320 grit sandpaper to get a nice smooth finish on the entire damaged area.

If you have a spray gun you can spray on gel coat or an undercoat and then a topcoat to get an appropriate finish. Painting is not easy, and getting a perfect color match often taxes even a professional. In fact, pros will often paint the entire side of the hull rather than a single area to get a color match. If you do not have a spray gun you can either ask a professional at your local yard to do it, or try using a new brushable topside paint called Toplac. Toplac paint is designed to be brushed onto the topsides, but it is fairly runny and you will have to be careful not to get runs in the paintwork. If you make a mistake, simply sand it back and have the yard do the work.

Aluminum boats are subject to corrosion caused by stray electric currents in the water. You can decrease the chance of corrosion by attaching blocks of zinc to the shaft strut. Aluminum hulls can be patched with epoxy/fiberglass patches, too. They don't usually last as long as patches on fiberglass boats, though, since metal expands and contracts at different rates than glass does.

▲ A spray gun will help make quicker work of repainting your hull.

Your engine needs constant loving care to keep it running smoothly. There are maintenance steps that you can take to make sure it's in tip-top condition at all times.

- ► Keep the belts snugly tightened. Loose engine belts begin to slip and eventually, to break. On outboards, this will shut down the alternators. On inboards and inboard/outboards, it will shut down the alternator, as well as the water pumps, and the power steering. You can tighten the belts yourself by adjusting a moveable pulley, but don't over-tighten. Belts should have about 3/8- to 1/2-inch of flex, depending on the length of the belt. When you check the belts, look out for frayed areas. Also check under the bottom of the belt for signs of belt dust. This shows that the belt is misaligned. If you have any questions, get a good engine mechanic to look at it or buy a new belt.

- ► Test the steering system for looseness or stickiness. Listen for unusual noises as you turn it.

- ► Keep the steering system well lubricated.

- ► Once a year (usually when you haul out the boat) check the oil in the lower unit of outboards and stern drives. It should be dark and clear. If it is murky and looks like milky coffee, it means that there is water in the unit and you should have a mechanic take a look at it. You should also take it to a repair shop if there are bits of metal in the oil, which may indicate that something is falling apart. You can add oil to the lower unit by unscrewing the oil filler screw on the bottom side of the gear housing and pumping oil into the filler hole. Make sure you wipe off any excess oil when you are done.

TIP

You can buy motor oil at your local discount retailer for half the price charged by outboard companies for brand-name oils. Look for oil rated TCW-3 by the Society of Automotive Engineers.

- ► Retighten all loose screws, nuts, and bolts when they begin to loosen. You will need a torque wrench for most engines.

► On older engines, check the spark plugs regularly. Replace chafed plug wires and make sure connecting insulation snaps securely on the spark plug contacts. Once a year, remove the spark plugs, clean them with a wire brush, and use a torque wrench to tighten them again.

► Inspect the propeller for bent blades. You may have to haul out your boat to check for damage, or you can use a mask and snorkel if you suspect something is wrong. Usually, the first sign of a problem is a vibration or repeated banging on the hull. Either one could mean that you've picked up a lobster pot warp and wrapped it around the prop. If the shaft is bent (from going aground or hitting a submerged object), you will hear the noise and feel vibrations.

► If your boat is suddenly losing speed as it goes off a wave, you may be feeling the prop ventilate. This means that the prop is not submerged deeply enough and air is being sucked down into the propeller. The solution may be to get a longer shaft outboard or install anti-ventilation plates (sometimes erroneously called anti-cavitation plates). You could also be getting loss of thrust from the prop cavitating, especially if the boat slows when it is running at high speed and the prop sounds as if it is turning improperly. Cavitation is caused by the prop turning too fast and creating a bubble of air in the water, almost like water boiling in a pot. When a prop cavitates, it loses thrust over the back of the blades. This leads to erratic performance at high speeds as the bubble forms and collapses.

► The effects of cavitation on the propeller can be seen by looking at the blade tips. If cavitation is present, the tips usually show signs of pitting and wear. They will also be very shiny. These pits are caused by the bubble of air on the back of the blade collapsing and reforming. Every time it collapses it takes a tiny bit of the prop material with it. On many high-speed engines you will see signs of cavitation on the prop, but only severe problems warrant changes. Ask your repair shop technician if you have any questions about your prop.

Boats used on salt water or for fishing should be washed down after use. Except for hard-to-remove dirt, all you need to use is dishwashing soap and water, or special boat-washing soap. You can scrub with a sponge on flat surfaces, but you'll need a brush on non-skid surfaces. If you wash the boat on the water, make sure you use a biodegradable soap. There are plenty on the market. The key to keeping your boat looking fresh and new is to wash and wax it regularly.

A bathroom cleaner spray works fine on spots. But don't use an abrasive cleaner, because it will ruin the gel coat of fiberglass.

To get rid of fishy smells and remains, clean the live wells with a diluted solution of bleach. Make sure you wash the bleach out very thoroughly with water, or the residue will kill your next catch.

Prevent mildew in cabins and other enclosed areas with mildew killers like Damp-Rid, No-Damp, and Lysol. On sunny days, bring cabin pads and pillows up to the deck to air out.

Once or twice a year, polish the gel coat with a boat wax. Do this by wiping wax over a small area and then rubbing it in with a circular motion. If you can use a puffing pad, so much the better, but do not polish one spot for too long. Never apply the wax to any surfaces where people will be walking. It will make the decks slippery.

> **Maintaining your boat** in tip-top condition can make a difference of up to 20% in the price you can sell it for when you decide to invest in a larger boat. Brokers usually tell you that the cleanest boat sells for the highest prices. So when you come to sell your boat, make sure it is cleaner than it has ever been before.

Lines

Like the rest of your boat, nylon lines should be washed off after each trip and dried in the sun. Stow them in a dry place to avoid mildew. Before storage, the lines need to be coiled. Coiling a line so that it remains tangle-free can be a tricky procedure. If it's a laid line, you'll want to coil it clockwise over your hand, giving each coil a half-twist to the right. Braided line is less likely to kink and you don't need to twist it. Once the rope is coiled, wrap the end of the rope counterclockwise around the coils and make a small loop of the left over end. Pass this end through the coils and then put the end of the rope through the loop and your coil is ready to store.

After it is cut, the bitter end of a line tends to unravel. To prevent this, tape the line where you are about to cut it and cut through the middle of the taped section. That way, neither side unravels. You can ask the store where you bought the nylon line to seal the ends. You can also buy a commercial paint-like product that seals the ends when you dip the rope in it. Alternatively, you can burn it with a soldering iron or a flame until the nylon melts. Then roll the end between two pieces of wood to round it off. Do not roll it with your fingers—the hot nylon will stick to your skin and can give you a painful burn.

Trailers

Your trailer will undergo a lot of wear and tear hauling your boat from storage to water and back again. Treat it well to get the longest use possible from it. Every time the trailer is backed into salt water, wash it down afterwards with a solution of soap and fresh water to prevent rust and corrosion. Spray the springs and bolts with a rustproofing spray. Allow the trailer to dry before going on the road with it or you may find that the brakes don't work because they are full of water.

TIP

Painted steel trailers are attractive but rust easily. If you plan to put your trailer in salt water, buy aluminum or galvanized steel.

Once a month, check the tire pressure. And before each long pull, grease the wheel bearings. You can lock grease fittings called Bearing Buddies into the wheel hub and add the grease when needed. The Buddies feed the grease into the inner and outer bearings. You'll need a grease gun to force grease into the hub at the bearing fittings. Finally, make sure all nuts on the winch and the hitch are secure and tightened regularly. All that rattling and banging causes them to loosen regularly.

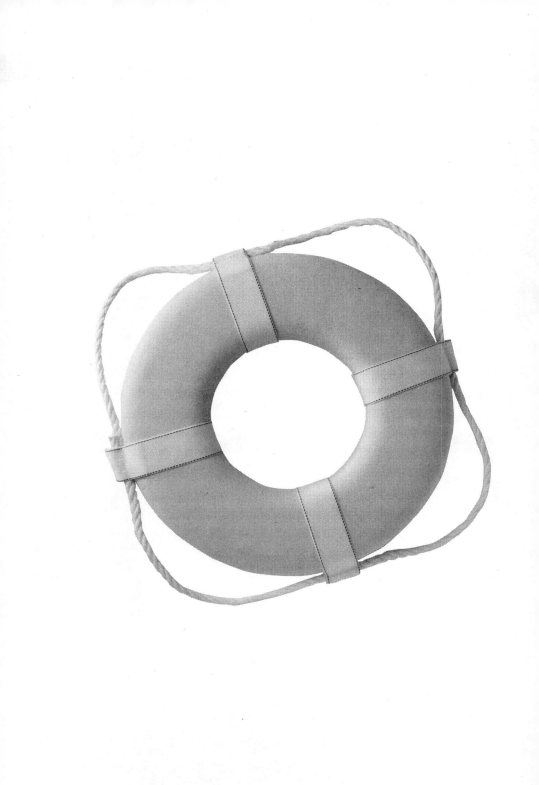

PART IV

TROUBLE-SHOOTING

I f you practice good seamanship procedures and maintain your boat, your powerboat experience should be relatively problem-free. But what do you do when something really goes wrong? Here are some of the most commonly asked questions about real emergencies—and some answers from the experts.

CHAPTER 12

EMERGENCY!

What do you do if there's real trouble? Despite all maintenance and the best laid plans of mice, men, and sailors, things can and do go wrong.

There are lots of reasons why your engine might not start. A few of them are:

- ► You forgot to put the key in the ignition and turn on the gas.

- ► You're out of fuel. Fuel gauges on boats are often inaccurate. Make sure that you always leave the dock with a full tank. Tow service operators get most of their calls from boats that have run out of fuel.

- ► The shift lever is not in neutral. Most marine engines don't start if they're already in gear.

- ► The battery is dead. You can use jumper cables from your auxiliary batteries to get the engine battery going, but many boats have a switch that allows you to use your house batteries to start the engines.

- ► The battery wires are loose. Wiggle them to see if they're tight and check for corrosion around the connectors. Scrape off the corrosion if you find any and retighten the wires.

- ► The fuse has blown. Replace it with the spare you carry on board.

- ► The gas is there, but no fuel is getting to the firing chamber. It could be that the fuel has run out of the carburetor because the motor was not stored in an upright position. You want to choke the engine by pressing in on the ignition key and cranking the starter. As soon as the motor turns over, stop choking or you may flood the engine. If it sputters to a stop, crank again. You might have to repeat the process a few times until the engine runs smoothly.

- ► You pulled the kill switch. Turn it back on.

- ► You may not have plugged in the Deadman's switch properly. (The switch with the curly wire that goes around your wrist to stop the engine if you fall off the boat.) Check it.

- ► There's an obstruction/dirt/water in the fuel line. Check to make sure that all fittings are attached, the hose is unobstructed, the vents are open, and the filters are clean.

- ► The engine runs but doesn't shift into gear. You may have something entangled in the propeller. Tilt up the lower unit and investigate.

If a fire starts on your boat, the first consideration must be for the passengers, so you should have a plan for abandoning ship if need be. If you have a gasoline explosion, there is usually little you can do except reach for a Personal Flotation Device (PFD) and go over the side.

If you don't have to abandon ship immediately, take the following steps as quickly as possible:

► Turn the boat so that the flames blow outboard, not inboard.

► Make a radio distress call, if time permits, giving the boat's location.

► Make sure the passengers move to the safest area of the boat, such as the bow, with their PFDs on.

► Reach for the appropriate fire extinguisher and fight the fire as described below.

▲ Pull out the extinguisher lock pin and squeeze the two handle levers together. Aim at the base of the flame with a sweeping motion; hold the stream steadily on the base of the flames until you are certain the fire is out. Dry chemical extinguishers are effective for 5 to 15 feet from the nozzle, Halon 1211 for 9 to 15 feet, Halon 1301 up to 6 feet, and CO_2 up to 3 feet.

Galley fires

According to most fire chiefs who have dealt with onboard fires, you should understand that if you cannot get the fire under control in a few minutes, you are likely to lose control of it altogether. As Chief Art Christman, of Jamestown, RI, says: "If you can't knock it down in a few minutes, get out of there. Your boat isn't worth your life." Boats are built of flammable materials such as wood, fiberglass, and paint, and they have flammable materials onboard such as fuel, oil, and cooking fuel. You need to have extinguishers handy in the galley ready for immediate use.

Fires in a galley are most likely to be fueled by flammable liquids such as grease, propane, or alcohol, or by combustible solid materials such as paper, wood, or fabric. A U.S. Coast Guard (USCG) Class A, B, or C extinguisher will be effective against most kinds of fires. If no extinguisher is available, use materials at hand such as a towel to beat out the flames. If you have time to soak the towel, that will be even better. Do not use water on grease or alcohol fires. If your stove uses propane for cooking, turn off the fuel supply from the tank. Once the fuel supply is cut off, let the fire burn itself out. If necessary, soak nearby wooden or fabric surfaces with water to keep the fire from spreading.

Gasoline, diesel oil, or grease fires

Use a Class B foam, CO2, or dry chemical extinguisher. Do not use water because it will only spread the flames.

Fires below deck

Fires in a vessel's cabins or lockers will most often be fueled by combustible material such as wood, paper, or fabric. You should have a Class A extinguisher mounted below, where you and your crew can get to it easily, even in the dark. If no Class A extinguisher is available, flood the fire's base with water and/or rob the fire of oxygen by closing a door or hatch to snuff it out.

Engine fires

Shut off all engines, generators, and fans sharing the engine space involved with the fire, then close any engine-room doors or hatches. If the engine-room fire extinguisher system has not discharged automatically, activate it manually. If your boat has a small, specially

designed aperture through which you can discharge your extinguisher without opening the engine compartment, do so as quickly as possible. Try not to
open the compartment, because this will admit oxygen and may cause the
flames to increase.

If you have one, get your crew to prepare the life raft and prepare to
launch it. Get the crew into life jackets. If there is time, transmit a Mayday
distress call on your portable. Don't stay below to use the Very High
Frequency (VHF) radio while a fire is raging.

Use any fire extinguisher and aim it at the base of the flames.

Electrical fires

Use an approved Class C fire extinguisher designed specifically for this purpose.
Never use water, because it conducts electricity. Fires in electrical-wiring
insulation cannot sustain themselves without a great deal of oxygen; if your
circuit panels are encased in a heavy metal box, closing the box may be
sufficient to extinguish the fire.

What do I do if my boat springs a leak?

If your boat springs a leak, turn on all electric bilge pumps immediately.
Then try to identify where the water is coming in. Most leaks in fiberglass
and aluminum boats will be caused by damage to through-hull fittings such
as hoses, keel bolts, underwater exhausts, and so on. Generally, your bilge
pump will be able to remove the water faster than it leaks in. If you prepared
your boat properly before you went to sea, you will have a suitably sized
bung tied to each through-hull fitting. If any of them let go, you will be able
to plug the leak with a bung and do everything possible to remove the
water. If you have a really big leak (say you have hit a submerged object),
stuff the hole with anything available, from cushions and pillows to bedding.
As quickly as possible, reinforce soft plug materials with something flat and
solid, such as a hatch cover, battens, or bed slats. The water should now
be coming into the boat more slowly than you're able to pump it out. If possible, hold a bed cover or jacket over the side of the boat and see if it
is sucked into the hole. This will help to plug the hole temporarily. If you
are near a beach or marina, head for it at once. If you can get your boat
aground, you know it won't sink. But if you start sinking, call for assistance.

Falling overboard is a common mishap on boats. Whether it turns into an emergency depends on how quickly action is taken. Every crew should conduct man-overboard (MOB) drills on a regular basis. The priority should be getting the boat near the victim as soon as possible so that the swimmer stays in sight of those on deck.

Here are the steps you should take:

► Shout "Man overboard" and keep eyes on the victim. Whoever sees the person go overboard should point at the person in the water and not lose sight of him or her. This crewperson should do nothing but point during the entire rescue.

► Turn off the power immediately.

► Throw the victim a cockpit cushion or life ring.

► Turn the boat toward the victim in a simple circle.

► Come in close to the victim, but no closer than 10 feet. Toss him or her a lifeline or lifesling. If the victim is able to swim, get a swim ladder over the side and help him or her aboard. If the victim is exhausted, injured, or unconscious, you will need two or three strong adults to lift him or her on board. If someone absolutely must go into the water to help, it is essential that he or she wear a PFD.

▲ Conduct MOB drills regularly.

WHAT TO DO IF YOU FALL OVERBOARD

Just as important as acquiring the skills necessary for rescuing a crew member overboard is knowing how to help yourself if you are the person overboard. The following tips can help you stay afloat until you are recovered.

- ▶ Keep your clothes on. If your shoes are light enough for you to swim in comfortably, leave them on. If they weigh you down, however, remove them. Remove any heavy objects from any pockets in your clothing.

- ▶ If you can float on your back fairly easily, save energy by doing so. Kick only when necessary.

- ▶ While signaling for help or waiting for rescue, tread water to stay in an upright position, moving your hands back and forth and using a kick that requires little energy. Remember, the more you move around in cold water, the quicker your body temperature can drop, and the faster hypothermia can set in.

- ▶ In warm water, conserve your energy by using the facedown floating technique, called survival floating. Each move you make should be slow and easy.

- ▶ Every second counts. As soon as a heaved line reaches you, quickly tie a bowline around your chest. If a Lifesling reaches you, slip it on immediately.

- ▶ As the rescue boat approaches, stay away from both the stern and the bow of the boat.

- ▶ When trying to board the boat, don't rush; it is important to make effective use of your remaining energy.

Hypothermia is a lowering of body temperature that can occur when someone has been in the cold for a long time. The body can no longer generate sufficient heat to maintain normal body temperature. It can happen if you fall into the water, sit in the cockpit for a while on a cold, windy day, or even just motor along on your boat in spring when the water and air are cool.

Mild hypothermia may include shivering and dizziness. Moderate hypothermia includes shivering, dizziness, a low, irregular pulse, irregular breathing, numbness, confusion, drowsiness, and apathy. The solution is to get the person warm immediately by putting him or her in a sleeping bag with another person or hot water bottles and getting medical attention as soon as possible.

Avoid shaking or shocking anyone with severe hypothermia. Get victims to a medical professional immediately. They must be warmed carefully or they will die. Get the victim out of the cold and into dry clothing. Wrap him or her in blankets and warm up the body slowly. Rapid rewarming can cause dangerous heart rhythms. Monitor vital signs and be prepared to give rescue breathing and CPR. Warm the victim until medical help arrives.

If you keep a weather eye open all the time you are at sea, you should not get caught in a storm. If you listen to the National Oceanic and Atmospheric Administration (NOAA) weather radio, unless your boat is really slow and you are a long, long way from shore, you will be able to get ashore before a storm hits. However, if you are caught by bad weather, take the following precautions:

- ► Secure all hatches and close all ports and windows.
- ► Remember that bilge water adversely affects a boat's stability. Pump bilges dry and repeat as required.
- ► Secure all loose gear. Put away small items and lash down the larger ones.
- ► At the first sign of weather worsening, make sure that everyone on board is wearing a PFD.
- ► Break out any emergency gear that you might need, such as hand pumps, bailers, or a drogue. You would use a drogue to keep the boat stern to the seas in really heavy weather or if you were going to try to cross a sandbar with breaking water to get into harbor.
- ► Check your position, if possible, and update the plot on your chart.
- ► Plan to alter your course to sheltered waters if necessary.
- ► Reassure your crew and guests. Instruct them what to do and what not to do, then assign each crewmember a task to take his or her mind off the situation.

A boat is "swamped" when it fills with water from over the side. Most small fiberglass boats have buoyancy built into them in the form of plastic foam flotation material. Use anything at hand to bail out the water, or hand-paddle to the nearest shore. A boat is "capsized" when it is knocked down so that it lies on its side in the water or turns over.

Many powerboats get swamped because the driver backs down hard, causing water to come over the transom at the outboard cut-out. If your boat has this feature and you will be sportfishing, build an extra transom board inside the outboard. That way, if you get swamped from astern, the secondary board will stop most of the water from coming inboard. Incidentally, a recent Boat/US survey found that over 30% of boat losses were caused by swamping over the transom in just this manner.

If you have a sportfishing boat and tend to back down hard while fighting a fish, you should make sure that all cockpit hatches are watertight and secured tightly before you start fishing. Also check that any wiring in the cockpit area is watertight.

Having capsized or swamped, it is important to remain calm and conserve energy. The general rule is to ensure that all crew members are wearing PFDs and that they stay with the boat. There may be opportunities for righting the boat, and rescuers will be able to find you more easily if you stay with your boat.

It happens to everyone sooner or later: you run aground. If you hit a soft bottom and there is no water coming into the bilge, try simply backing out. If that doesn't work and you suspect you are on a mud bank, try blasting over the top of it. If you try to run around 180 degrees there's a good chance you'll ground your struts or props and be there until high tide comes along. On small boats you can turn around with a pole or an oar. If the water is shallow enough, simple solutions like getting everybody out of the boat will let the boat float free. Then you can try to push the boat off.

If that doesn't work, try getting everyone on one side of the boat to heel it over. Often it is only the keel that is stuck and heeling the boat works. Another technique is to take an anchor out in the direction that you went aground in and set it firmly as far away astern from the boat as the anchor line will let you. You may be able to lead the line to your windlass and crank the boat aftwards off the sandbar. If nothing else, setting an anchor out will keep you from being driven further aground. If you go aground on a river, it is often possible to take an anchor line to a nearby tree and haul yourself off, using the bow windlass or capstan with the outboard fully raised.

TIP

To keep your boat from running aground, study your charts!

Yet another trick is to use the boat's props to blast a channel in the mud of the seabottom. By running your engine in forward or astern, you might be able to use the thrust from the props as excavators to deepen the seabed locally. Of course, it will stir up a lot of silt, but you may get free.

If you hit a rocky bottom at speed, the first thing you should do is check for hull damage and make any temporary repairs you can. Typically, you will rip the props (with inboards) and quite possibly the shafts right out of the bottom of the boat. Outboards and stern drives will probably suffer lower end and prop damage. But don't worry—the boat will be high and dry and is unlikely to sink much further. (Unless you go right over the rocks and sink the boat on the other side.) At this point you must consider how to get your boat salvaged or towed off the rocks.

I need to be towed

If the tide is falling or a storm is rising and your boat is stuck somewhere, it may be time to consider getting towed. You can call for a commercial towing service on your VHF channel 16. Or you can contact a passing boat. Make sure you understand the salvage forms and the relevant laws. There have been cases in which boat owners who were not members of a towing organization were charged hundreds of dollars and threatened with the potential loss of their boat because they allowed the towing vessel to treat it as a salvaged boat. When a towing vessel arrives, offer your towing line and secure the tow line to the bow eye of your boat. Don't forget to tilt your drive out of the water if you have an outboard motor. If you have an inboard motor and can't tilt it, you may want to wait for a higher tide.

If you are contacted to help tow someone off the rocks, make sure you know what your liabilities are. There have been cases in which the boat owners tried to sue the boaters who towed them off the rocks for damage done in the process.

TIP
If you need a towing service, contact TowBoat/U.S., 800-888-4869. Or call Sea Tow, 631-765-3660.

HOW DO I TRANSMIT A PAN-PAN CALL?

Send a Pan-Pan (pronounced pahn-pahn) call on VHF channel 16 or 2182 kHz (SSB) when you have a "very urgent" but not life-threatening emergency:

1. "PAN-PAN . . . PAN-PAN . . . PAN-PAN

2. ALL STATIONS.

3. THIS IS (boat name) . . .(boat name). . .(boat name). . . .

4. WE (nature of your emergency).

5. WE REQUIRE (type of assistance required or other useful information such as your position, a description of your vessel, and the number of people on board).

6. (Boat name).

7. OVER."

HOW DO I CANCEL A PAN-PAN CALL?

If you decide you no longer require assistance, you must cancel the message:

1. "PAN-PAN, PAN-PAN.

2. HELLO ALL STATIONS, HELLO ALL STATIONS.

3. THIS IS (boat name).

4. TIME IS (time of transmission by 24-hour clock).

5. CANCEL PAN-PAN. OUT."

HOW DO I TRANSMIT A MAYDAY CALL?

Mayday calls are the most serious radio distress calls you can make and should be transmitted only in a life-threatening emergency. That means your ship is sinking in a storm, a crew member has had a heart attack, or there is a serious fire onboard. Running out of gas doesn't qualify. Issue the call on VHF Channel 16 or 2182 kHz (SSB). You will probably have to calm yourself down to speak clearly. Try not to yell or garble your words:

1. MAYDAY. . .MAYDAY. . .MAYDAY.

2. THIS IS (boat name). . .(boat name). . .(boat name). . ."

3. MAYDAY (boat name) POSITION IS (vessel position in degrees and minutes of latitude NORTH or SOUTH and longitude EAST or WEST, or as a distance and magnetic or true bearing from a well-known navigation landmark).

4. WE (nature of your emergency).

5. WE REQUIRE (type of assistance required).

6. ON BOARD ARE (number of adults and children on board AND safety equipment aboard). (State conditions of any injured).

7. (Boat name) IS A (boat length in feet)-FOOT (type) WITH A (hull color) HULL and (trim color) TRIM.

8. I WILL BE LISTENING ON CHANNEL (16 or 2182), THIS IS (boat name). OVER.

The act of abandoning ship is filled with potential hazards and should be undertaken only if your vessel is completely on fire or is in imminent danger of sinking. In many cases, even vessels that have been seriously damaged will remain afloat for hours or even days. Abandon ship only as a last resort. Try not to get into the water and swim to the life raft. It is very difficult to get into a raft from the water.

- As soon as you wonder if you might have to abandon ship, make certain that all crew members are warmly dressed and wearing PFDs.

- Instruct a trained crew member to stand by the life raft and prepare to launch it.

- Before you decide to abandon ship, transmit a Mayday distress call and message. If no one responds, do it again. If there is still no response, try other channels.

- Gather emergency supplies. If you're boating offshore, an abandon-ship bag includes signaling equipment, medical supplies, provisions, including a half-gallon of fresh water per person, clothing, and fishing supplies, and an EPIRB.

- Make certain that your raft is tethered to the boat, and then launch it. Have one crew member board.

- Load the rest of your crew into the life raft and have them fend it off from your vessel while you load your emergency gear.

- Activate your EPIRB as soon as you enter the raft and leave it activated. DO NOT turn it off for any reason. Searchers will use it to home in on you.

- If your boat is on fire or about to sink, cut the lines tethering the raft to it. But if it is merely awash, keep the raft tethered to the boat as long as possible, playing out the full length of the raft's tether.

- According to experts, the first thing that will happen when you get into the life raft is that you will become seasick. Even if you have a strong stomach, take a seasickness pill before getting into a life raft.

Glossary of Selected Terms

A-B

Aft: Near or at the stern.

Anchor rode: A line, chain, or steel cable used to hold a vessel fast to the anchor.

Astern: The direction toward the stern of a vessel, or beyond the stern.

Berth: (1) A place to sleep in a vessel; (2) a margin of safety, as a "wide berth."

Bilge: The lowest point of a vessel's interior hull; also the part of the exterior between the **bottom** and topsides, the "turn of the bilge."

Bottom: The underwater terrain used for anchoring.

Bow: The forward part of a boat.

Bow chocks: Fittings on a vessel's rail, near its bow, having jaws that serve as fairleads for anchor rodes and other lines.

Bowrider runabout: a runabout with additional seating in the bow accessed via a walk-through windshield; no formal sleeping accommodations, but seats may fold down for napping or sunning.

Bridge: The control station of a vessel; the persons in charge of a vessel, or (by extension) of an organization, such as the U.S. Power Squadron; a structure over water to carry pedestrian, vehicular or railroad traffic.

Broach to, broaching: The sudden, unplanned, and uncontrolled turning of a vessel so that the hull is broadside to the seas or to the wind.

Buoy: A floating aid to navigation showing channels or otherwise indicating location, rocks and other obstructions, and prohibited areas on the water; turning points in races; to buoy an anchor is to temporarily fasten the anchor line to a float, so that the anchor need not be raised when a vessel is leaving its anchorage.

Burgee: A special flag flown on a vessel or on a flagstaff of a shore installation, indicating either the ownership of the vessel or the identity of a yacht club or similar organization.

C

Can: A cylindrical buoy, generally green, sometimes black.

Capstan: A vertical winch on a deck, used for hauling, such as the anchor line.

Catamaran: A twin-hulled vessel, sail or power.

Cavitate, cavitation: Turbulence in the water caused by rotation of a propeller; causes wear on the propeller and a reduction in propeller efficiency.

Center console boat: A sportsboat popular with anglers because it provides maximum usable deck space.

Chandlery: Items of nautical gear or the shop where these are sold.

Chock: A rigging fitting, essentially shaped like a U or an O, normally mounted on the deck or in the toe rail, to control a rigging or mooring line.

Cleat: A rigging fitting to which mooring lines and miscellaneous lines are temporarily attached.

Compass card: The rotating dial on a compass.

Crazing: A fine network of cracks in the surface glaze of a boat.

Cuddy cabin: A small, austere cabin in the forward part of a boat.

D

Deep-vee racing craft: Boats with a V-shaped hull, designed for increased wave-riding and planing ability, and high speed.

Dinghy: A small boat used as a tender; the term is also used for a small racing sailboat.

Displacement: The weight of the water displaced by a floating hull; the volume of water will vary depending on whether it is fresh water or seawater.

Downwind: The direction to leeward, with the wind.

Draft: The vertical distance from the waterline to the lowest point of the hull or attachments such as propellers and rudders; thus, a minimum depth of water in which a vessel will float; a vessel is said to "draw" a certain amount of water.

E-F

Electrolysis: Stray current erosion that causes weakening of through-hull fittings; may result in safety hazards.

Express cruiser: A stylish, usually high-powered sportboat up to 40 feet long.

Fender: A cushioning device hung between the boat and a float, pier or another craft.

Flare: (1) A pyrotechnic signal that can indicate distress; (2) the outward curvature of the topsides.

Float plan: Detailed information on the boat, its crew, passengers and destination; usually given to a responsible relative or friend before departure.

Fluke: The flat, palm-shaped or shovel-shaped part of an anchor (on the end of each arm) that digs in to the bottom to prevent dragging.

Flying bridge: A high steering position, usually above the normal wheelhouse of a power cruiser; also called flybridge.

Foredeck: The forward part of the main deck or vessel.

Forward: On board a vessel, the direction to the front, toward the bow.

Freeboard: The vertical distance between the waterline and the top of the deck.

G

Galley: The kitchen on a boat or ship.

Gimbals: Pivoted rings holding a compass or other device so that it can tip in any direction or remain level when the support tips.

Global Positioning System (GPS): A worldwide radio-navigation system of high accuracy using orbiting satellites; designed and operated by the U.S. Department of Defense.

Ground tackle: Anchor, anchor rode (line or chain), and all the shackles and other gear used for attachment.

H

Hatch: A deck opening providing access to the space below; normally a hatch cover, hinged or sliding, if fitted.

Hauling out: Removing a boat from the water; pulling on an anchor line or a rope or line is simply called hauling.

Haul out: Removing a vessel from a boatyard for maintenance or storage.

Head: The bow or forward part of a vessel; the upper end of the vertical part, such as a rudder head; the toilet aboard ship.

Helm: The tiller, wheel, and other steering gear; a boat is said to have a weather helm if it tends to turn its bow to windward, lee helm if it tends to fall away to leeward.

Hull: The structural body of a vessel, not including superstructure, masts or rigging.

I-J-K-L

Idler pulley: Device used to tighten the slack in a fan belt.

Inboard: More toward the center of the vessel; inside; a motor fitted inside the boat.

Intracoastal Waterways (ICW): Bays, rivers and canals along coasts (such as Atlantic and Gulf of Mexico coasts), connected so vessels may travel without entering an open sea.

Keel: The main structural member of a vessel, the backbone; the longitudinal area beneath the hull that provides steering stability and reduces leeway.

Laid line: A three-strand rope with strands twisted clockwise in a right-hand lay.

List: A continuous leaning to one side, often caused by an imbalance in stowage or a leak into one compartment.

M-N

Mark-one eyeball: A keen nautical eye.

Mooring: Permanent ground tackle; a place where vessels are kept at anchor.

National Oceanic and Atmospheric Administration (NOAA): Provides the latest marine weather forecasts on weather radio channels.

Nun buoys: Buoys that are cylindrical to just above the waterline, where they taper to a conical top; usually red.

O-P

Osmosis: The seepage of seawater through the gel coat of a vessel; eventually causes osmotic blistering.

Outboard: (1) A propulsion system for boats, attached at the transom; includes motor, driveshaft, and propeller; fuel tank and battery may be integral or could be installed separately in the boat; (2) outside or away from a vessel's hull; opposite of inboard.

Personal flotation device (PFD): Any of several articles, such as buoyant cushions and vests or coats, "horseshoes," or life preserver rings.

Pitch: (1) The alternating rise and fall of the bow of a vessel proceeding through waves; (2) the theoretical distance advanced by a propeller in one revolution; (3) tar and resin used for caulking between the planks of a wooden vessel.

Planing hull: A hull designed so that forward speed creates water lift, reducing friction and increasing speed.

Production boats: Inexpensive boats made on production lines like cars and trucks; usually of fiberglass material.

Project boat: A fixer-upper.

Propeller (or rop): A rotating device with two or more blades that acts as a screw in propelling a vessel.

Pulpit: The forward railing structure at the bow of a boat.

R-S

Range: The difference between the high water level and the following low water level, or vice versa.

Rudder: The control surface, usually aft, by which a boat is steered.

Runabout: A powerboat with no formal sleeping accommodations; usually seats 4 or 6.

Saloon: Interior space at the level of the cockpit in sedan or convertible cruisers.

Sedan cruiser: Convertible powerboat.

Semi-displacement hull: Combines round-bottom sections forward and flat-bottom sections in the aft run for greater speed with a trade-off in fuel efficiency; sometimes referred to as semi-planing hull.

Slip: (1) A berth for a boat between two piers, floats, or piles; (2) the percentage difference between the theoretical and the actual distance that a propeller advances when turning in water under load.

Safety of Life at Sea (SOLAS): International boating safety organization that sets standards for life rafts, size capacity ratings, seaworthiness, and sturdiness; these conventions are adapted for the U.S. by the U.S. Coast Guard.

Stanchion: A metal post used to hold lifelines along a deck.

Stern: The afterportion of the boat.

Styrene: For polystyrene, a synthetic material used in some molded hulls.

T-U-V

Topsides: (1) The sides of a vessel above the waterline; (2) on deck as opposed to below deck.

Transom: The traverse part of the stern.

Trawler: Any pleasure craft more than 25 feet in length that does not carry sufficient horsepower to lift itself out of the water and plane at or near the surface.

Trim, trimmed: (1) The way in which a vessel floats, on an even keel, or trimmed by the head (bow) or stern, for example; adjustable by shifting ballast.

Trim tab: Rectangular control flaps that project parallel to the water's surface at the transom when the hull is planing; used to control the angle of the boat.

U.S. Coast Guard (USCG): The federal marine law enforcement and rescue agency in the U.S.

Vector chart: A chart plotting the predicted motion of the boat and the water during boat travel.

W-X-Y-Z

Wake: The track in the water of a moving vessel; commonly used for the disturbance of the water (waves) resulting from the passage of the vessel's hull.

Windlass: A special form of winch, a rotating drum device for hauling a line or chain.

Yacht broker: Agent working on behalf of the seller or buyer to sell or buy a boat, usually through a commission-based transaction.

Index